Mexican Cooking

CLASSIC DISHES, REGIONAL SPECIALITIES, AND TEX-MEX FAVORITES

BY KATHLEEN DUNNING FISHER

this book has been
Donated
in
Loving
Memory
of

Candace Lyn Johnson

GROSSET
GOOD LIFE
BOOKS

PUBLISHERS • GROSSET & DUNLAP • NEW YORK
A FILMWAYS COMPANY

Acknowledgments

Photographs on the following pages courtesy of the Mexican National Tourist Council: iv, 14, 63. Photographs on the following pages courtesy of the American Spice Trade Association: 17, 20, 28, 47 (bottom), 51, 52 (right), 53 (right), 57.

Cover photograph and all others by Mort Engel

Grateful acknowledgment is due to Ralph and Midalma, proprietors of Fonda Los Milagros Mexican Restaurant in New York for allowing us to photograph the preparation of many of the dishes in this book. Props for studio shots were kindly donated by Fred Leighton, Imports, Ltd., of New York City.

My deepest thanks to Lillie Stuckey of Lewis & Neale, Inc. Without her most generous help and wise counseling, I would never have completed this book.

My sincere thanks, too, to Beatriz Diaz, of the Mexican National Tourist Council.
Finally, I would like to express my gratitude to Gebhardt's Mexican Foods, who have been extremely kind in providing much useful material for this book.

For Jean, who loves Mexican food

Contents

¡Salud y Buen Comer! Good Health and Good Eating   5

1 Appetizers   21
2 Soups: "Wet" and "Dry"   27
3 Eggs   32
4 Corn   35
5 Fish   46
6 Poultry   50
7 Meat   56
8 Chili con Carne   61
9 Vegetables   65
10 Sauces and Salads   73
11 Desserts   79
12 Beverages   89
Sources of Supply   93
Index   94

A view of Santa Priscia, in Taxco, considered one of the most beautiful colonial churches in Mexico.

¡Salud y Buen Comer!
Good Health
and Good Eating

Have you ever noticed that Mexico on the map looks like a cornucopia? Perhaps this is symbolic of a country that has contributed so many of its native foods to enrich and delight the people of the Old World as well as the New.

When Captain Hernán Cortés and his men landed at a point in the Gulf of Mexico on their voyage from Spain in 1519, they were looking for gold. They found it in large quantities and looted enthusiastically. Other treasures that they discovered, however, were quite unexpected. They were introduced for the first time to new and delicious foods cooked by the native Indians with skill acquired through the centuries. Those ancient Aztecs served the Spanish *conquistadores* such delicacies as avocado, corn, a chocolate beverage made from the native cacao bean, delicious vanilla-flavored desserts, peanuts, tomatoes, chilies, squash, assorted beans and wild turkey, as well as papaya, pineapple and mango. All these foods constituted a totally new experience for the white men. They also tasted for the first time the vegetable we now know as the Irish potato, which is thought to have originated in Peru.

The Spaniards continued to be amazed at the degree of civilization and sophistication of the people they had conquered. The emperor Montezuma, so historians of that era wrote, dined from a choice of wild turkey, quail, partridge, duck and other game served on fine quality dishes set on tables covered with snowy white cloths. Meals ended with foamy hot chocolate served in gold cups with tortoiseshell spoons. Knives, too, were used at these meals, though forks, as in Europe, did not appear until much later.

The introduction of new foods was not all one-sided, however. The Spaniards carried with them oil, cinnamon, cloves, rice, wheat, peaches, apricots, sugar cane and live cattle. These were adopted readily by the Indians, and by good fortune both the wheat and the sugar cane thrived in this new environment, and so did the cattle. Wheat and sugar led to the creation of the famous Mexican sweet rolls, cakes, pastries and candy, for which we owe a debt of gratitude to the monastic orders of those days. Nuns and friars labored diligently and with dedication to the development and refining of many good dishes we enjoy today. Their pastries, crullers, custards, pancakes, fritters, jelly pastes such as guava and other fruits, and vanilla-flavored cookies quickly became a part of the Mexican cuisine we include today among our favorite foods.

As the cattle thrived, milk and cheese gradually became a part of the native cooking, and later a successful leather industry from the tanning of hides developed.

The Spanish cuisine, which mingled happily with native Mexican foods, had itself been influenced by foreign invasions of Spain. The early Romans certainly left their imprint, to be followed later by seven hundred years of Arab rule from the eighth to the fifteenth centuries.

These diverse cultures all fused to bring us what we know as the lively, flavorful dishes of Mexico. Well-to-do Mexicans were exposed to French food during the brief and tragic reign of Maximilian and Carlota in the 1860s. Today in the houses of the upper-income groups and in luxury hotels and restaurants, the menus still have a European accent. Most of the people, however, cling to the favorites enjoyed by their ancestors—tortillas, tacos, enchiladas, tamales and beans.

While Mexico developed cooking as an art, it also gained the distinction of being the first country in North America to start the restaurant business. On December 1, 1525, the mayor and city council of Mexico City authorized a settler, Pedro Hernández Paniagua, to open an inn by declaring that they had granted a license "for setting up an inn in his houses where he can receive those who may come there and may also sell them bread and wine and other necessary things for which he shall keep a schedule of prices for the things which he sells and shall comply with it."

Principal roads had already established houses to offer food and shelter to travelers, but this was the first time that regulations had been issued. The rules indicate the Spaniards' adherence to the law, a trait still in evidence today.

Since tourism is important to the Mexican economy, hotels and restaurants have mushroomed over the years, to appeal both to the "carriage trade" as well as to the traveler in more modest circumstances. No matter what you are willing to spend, however, you will find a smiling, friendly people who really mean it when they say "bienvenido" or welcome!

While many of us tend to think of Mexican food as being too hot and spicy for our taste, we can always modify the seasoning to suit us. There is no law that says you have to follow a recipe exactly when it comes to spices, and it isn't necessary to burn your tongue when you want to bring the flavor of Mexico to your table. So let's live adventurously and enjoy some favorite dishes of our neighbors south of the border.

That Mexican cooking has gained widespread popularity is apparent at the White House. President Johnson was well known for throwing Tex-Mex barbeques, and his fondness for south-of-the-border cooking was shared by the Nixons. Since they had lived so close to the border, they had developed a taste for some of the better-known Mexican dishes and introduced them in the White House staff restaurant. Soon it became the custom to serve a Thursday luncheon "special" of enchiladas, *chiles rellenos,* tacos, rice with chili, and *guacamole* (avocado salad). Since Thursday comes only once a week, though, the navy cooks who service this restaurant found it was a smart idea to have at least one "short order" item every day, such as tacos or "two alarm" chili. Let the senators order their famous bean soup, the White House staffers would stay with their piquant, flavorful Mexican dishes.

The Mexican Kitchen

Country kitchens in Mexico today still include equipment used at the time of the *conquistadores*—such as hollowed-out gourds and the *molcajete* or mortar and pestle for grinding spices, fashioned out of rough, volcanic rock. The *metate,* also of volcanic rock, is a slanting, rectangular slab on three sturdy legs that is used with a *mano,* which looks like a crude rolling pin. The *metate* is used for the back-breaking job of grinding corn, chilies and the cacao bean, all of them needed for the ever popular sauces and the preparation of *masa,* the corn dough that is the staff of life to the average Mexican. *Cazuelas* or casseroles are plentiful, for they are used daily. Made of clay, they usually come in colorful and beautiful designs that demonstrate the artistic talents and love of beauty of the Mexicans.

While the country kitchen may be an artist's

The molinillo *is used to beat hot chocolate to a delicious froth.*

dream, city cooks usually prefer today's labor-saving devices and make good use of the electric blender and other up-to-date equipment. A tortilla press may prove to be a good investment if you are really dedicated to Mexican food, and understandably many of us are "hooked" after our first visit to Mexico. In every town and village you can watch the street vendors of tortillas—women who break off a small piece of *masa* or cornmeal dough and flatten it rapidly as they pat it between the palms of both hands to almost paper thinness. They work rapidly with a skill passed on through centuries. We don't urge American homemakers to attempt this. The tortilla press, which works quickly and efficiently, consists of two metal disks about seven inches in diameter, fastened together with a hinge. Each disk has a handle to use for opening and closing the press. After the tortilla has been shaped, it is baked on a *comal,* a flat clay or cast-iron griddle.

The *molinillo,* or beater, is a wooden implement with a handle about fifteen inches long and a fancifully carved knob or series of knobs at one end. It is used for beating the daily hot chocolate. The handle is rotated rapidly between the palms of the hands to give the required amount of foam. The bean masher is useful in preparing beans as a spread for tostados or tacos, but it is so similar to our wooden potato masher that the two can be interchanged.

The American kitchen is usually supplied with enough equipment to produce closely the textures of authentic Mexican dishes. The electric blender is, of course, almost a "must," while a heavy cast-iron griddle will substitute for the *comal.* The tortilla press may be obtained from many gourmet and specialty shops or Chinese stores, which use them for shaping their own pancakes, as well as stores specializing in Spanish foods. The *molinillo* offers no problem. You can use an ordinary egg beater until the chocolate is foamy enough for your taste. Just be careful not to spatter!

So you see, "going Mexican" does not mean any great outlay for new equipment. Just use what you have on hand.

Foods and Flavors of Mexico

Corn

Without a doubt, corn can be considered the

Corn kernels in the molcajete, *a mortar and pestle made from volcanic rock.*

Four textures of the ubiquitous corn.

most important grain in the Mexican diet. We know it was greatly prized by the ancient Toltecs, who preceded the Aztecs and the Mayas. The Mayas in turn considered it their most valuable food, as did the Aztecs. Archaeologists now have evidence that it was grown in the area we know as Mexico as far back as 6000 B.C.

There was an aura of mysticism about corn. Since it helped to nourish and sustain the living, it was regarded as a life symbol, a sacred plant that was evident in all social and religious life. The Toltecs, who flourished between the sixth and eighth centuries, had a legend that their most important god, Quetzalcoatl, helped them discover corn. Because of jealousy he had to leave them but promised to return. This legend was largely responsible for the warm welcome that Cortés received from the Aztecs when he arrived. They thought he was the god who had promised to return and treated him as such. The murder of Montezuma and the subsequent enslavement of his people are probably the most horrifying abuses of hospitality in all history.

Corn, which remains the staff of life today in the Mexican diet, is used to make the flour for *masa,* the dough common to tortillas, enchiladas, tostados, tacos and other dishes. The corn kernels are first soaked in lime water. In addition to softening the corn for grinding, the lime also adds valuable calcium, which may help explain the beautiful teeth of Mexicans. After soaking, the mixture is brought to a boil and then cooled. The liquid is later drained off and the kernels are rubbed between the hands to get rid of the outer skin. The result is now called *nixtamal.* After the *nixtamal* is blended with water, it is ready for grinding to a smooth paste on the *metate.* If all this sounds bothersome—it is! It's much simpler to purchase the commercial product, known as *masa harina,* which is distributed by the Quaker Oats Company. You can buy it in Spanish groceries and specialty stores or by mail (see page 93 for Sources of Supply).

Chilies

When Peter Piper picked a peck of pickled peppers, what he picked should never have been called peppers. The early Spanish explorers, when they landed in the Caribbean area, were actually looking for a shorter route to the riches of the East, namely spices.

Even in those days, pepper was by far the most valuable spice. So when the Spaniards found little red vegetable pods that the Indians used in cooking to impart a "bite" to their food, they named them peppers. This may have been an innocent mistake on their part or a bit of face saving. In any case, the misnomer "pepper" has come down through the ages, even though what we now call chili peppers are, from the botanist's point of view, members of the capsicum family.

Better get to know them, as they are an integral part of the Mexican cuisine. Because the climate varies so much in different parts of the country, from remote mountain regions to lush, tropical lowlands, Mexico produces many kinds of chilies. One expert, in fact, estimates there are at least one hundred varieties in Mexico. So we will turn our attention to just a few of the most commonly used types and skip the rest.

Chile serrano: This small green pepper, about 1½ inches long, has a strong, fresh flavor and is one of the most popular chilies. It is often served in a small dish so that everyone can select enough to chop into soup, rice or meat. It is also served chopped in *guacamole.* The *chile serrano* adds flavor when cooked with rice, but be careful not to break it. The seeds are so hot you would need a mouth made of asbestos.

Chile jalapeño: This dark green pepper, about 2½ inches long, is popular in central Mexico and Veracruz and is often served stuffed with fish or cheese. Be wary of the seeds, though. They are fiery. Available here in cans, they are generally packed *"en escabeche,"* that is, with oil, vinegar and herbs.

Chile poblano: This is the chili from Puebla, and it resembles our green bell pepper except that it is hot to the taste. It will behave well if properly treated, however. California cooks, who probably have easier access to supplies of this pepper than cooks in the rest of the country, have developed their own easy way of preparing them. To make quick work of removing the outer skin, they first wash and dry

the peppers and then place them in a shallow pan. Next they place them under the broiler, about 5 or 6 inches from the source of heat, until the skin blisters. The peppers then go into a paper bag, and the top is twisted to close it. After 15 minutes, they are removed from the bag and placed under the cold-water faucet. The skin then comes off in a jiffy. Simple!

Dried Chilies

Chile ancho: This is probably the chili most commonly used by Mexican cooks. Deep reddish-brown in color, it ranges in flavor from mild to fairly hot. Often ground, it is then used to make the base of a cooked sauce. Available in Mexican and specialty foods stores.

Cascabel: A small, round, smooth pepper with red-brown skin and nutty flavor, it varies in degree of heat.

New Mexico chili: As the name implies, this pepper is available in the United States. It is reddish-black, elongated, and mild to very hot in flavor.

California green chili: The name is appropriate, for that is what it is, California's version of a green Mexican chili, varying from mild to mildly hot.

A word of caution. After handling dried chilies, always wash your hands with soap and water to avoid a burning sensation on the skin. If you are extrasensitive, better wear plastic gloves when handling them.

You can substitute local varieties for many of these peppers if they are unavailable in your area. Although you might not achieve the exact flavor of a true Mexican dish, you'll find it is fun to experiment and exert your culinary skill and imagination. Our green bell pepper will do a sturdy job as understudy for *chilies rellenos* (stuffed peppers). Chances are you already have a favorite recipe for them anyway. Then if you want more of a Mexican touch, why not turn to the chili powder that's on every supermarket shelf? All right, it may not have the true Mexican flavor, but it will be delicious anyhow. It seems as though we live in an age of convenience, and particularly convenience foods. We may as well take advantage of our age and use chili powder, which really falls into this category. While it is a product of our own Southwest, chili powder gives us a taste of Old Mexico, for it contains the heat of chili peppers blended with many other spices such as cumin, oregano and garlic, and depending on the manufacturer, it may also include ground cloves, allspice and powdered onion.

Tomatoes

A native of Mexico, the tomato has a name that comes from *tomatl,* the Aztec word for a small green tomato that is still flourishing today, and *xictl,* the red variety so familiar to us now (it's better not to try to pronounce them; you'll sound as though you had hiccups). By combining the two words, Mexicans somehow arrived at *jitomate,* and that's what it is—our familiar, luscious, red tomato. Over the years, the Mexican government has done a great deal to improve agriculture, and so the varieties we know today probably bear little resemblance to those of years past.

When the Spaniards brought the tomato back to Europe, it got a very mixed reception, mostly bad. Botanists knew that it belonged to the solanacea family, and since some of its relatives were harmful, the general public regarded the tomato as poisonous.

Spanish monks, nevertheless, adopted it and encouraged its cultivation. We have ample evidence of their industry, for many of their recipes date back to 1740. It took another hundred years for the French to accept the tomato, and even then they were suspicious. The name they gave it, *pomme d'amour,* or love apple, did nothing to endear it to the French housewife who naturally thought anything with such a name must be an aphrodisiac. At first they used only the juice; then when nobody dropped dead or turned into a sex maniac, they gradually began to use the entire fruit.

Perhaps because of its refreshing flavor and its nutritional value, the tomato is now one of the most widely used agricultural products throughout the world. High in vitamin C, with traces of valuable copper to help the body absorb iron, and low in calories, it is the dieter's delight.

The tomatoes grown in Mexico are of especially fine quality, and their ready acceptance has made them one of that country's major exports. There is a very special place for tomatoes in the Mexican cuisine. Aside from their colorful addition to soups, salads, sauces and main dishes, they help transform the somewhat aggressive flavor of those ever present chilies into a smooth, though still lively, blend.

Beans

Beans are as close to the Mexican cuisine as our tradition of steak and potatoes is to ours. There is an astonishing variety available to the Mexican cook, in a wide range of colors, flavors, sizes and shapes. Most popular are the *frijol negro* (black bean), the speckled pinto, the red kidney bean and the *frijol canario,* a pale yellow bean.

As part of the filling for tacos, tortillas, enchiladas and other favorites, cooked beans are also served as a separate and rather soupy vegetable after the meat course. For extra zip, many Mexicans add a little grated cheese to melt into them or a chopped, pickled chili.

While beans are the staple food of the poor, they are enjoyed by everyone. Since Mexicans on the whole eat less meat than we do, beans, especially when used with cheese, make a valuable addition of protein to the diet. Surely there is a lesson we can learn here when we want to reduce the high cost of the weekly food bill.

You will find *frijoles refritos* (refried beans) on nearly every menu that claims to be truly Mexican, for this is a standard favorite. You might think from the name that the beans are fried twice, but they really only make one trip to the skillet. The beans have already been cooked in a clay pot or casserole; then they are heated in lard and mashed on the *comal* or griddle before serving.

We can use some pointers on the preparation of beans from knowledgeable cooks of Mexican foods. Diana Kennedy, who has written one of the most comprehensive books, *The Cuisines of Mexico,* advises us not to soak beans overnight for the best flavor. She also tells us to cook the beans very slowly. With the rebirth of the crock pot in this country, it now seems like a good time to use it. Cooking time can vary considerably from 1½ to 2½ hours, depending on how dry the beans are. Never add salt until the beans are cooked. Mexicans say it hardens the skins, and you may also remember that this rule applies when cooking peas and corn on the cob. Salting comes at the end of the cooking time for the same reason. Mrs. Kennedy continues with the suggestion that beans have a much better flavor if cooked in an earthenware pot—another good reason for bringing out the crock pot.

Finally, beans taste better if eaten a day or so after cooking. Be sure to refrigerate them as soon as they are cool, however. They will spoil quickly if left at room temperature. You can keep them for several days in the refrigerator if you bring them to a boil each day and then let them cool, just the same as you would treat soup stock.

Garbanzos are the legumes we know as chick peas. They are readily available in cans here, as are the red kidney beans.

Rice

While rice is not a native of Mexico, it has been so well adapted to the Mexican cuisine that we tend to look on the many dishes with rice as truly Mexican.

In the 1560s the Spanish trade routes to the Far East were being threatened by the Portuguese and Turks, so the Spaniards were obliged to open up new passages using the Phillippines as their chief source of supplies. Manila was founded and soon became a clearinghouse for Oriental spices, foods, silks and other luxuries. So in this fashion the Spaniards obtained rice and brought it from Manila to Acapulco, where it made its successful bow. Mexican cooks, with their imaginative skills, quickly developed their own savory way of preparing this new food, and their rice dishes appear to be endless, each with its individual personality.

Arroz, or rice served alone, is considered a "dry" soup (*sopa seca*) and is often used as a course by itself, usually after the "wet" soup (*sopa aguada*). It can also be eaten with tortillas and perhaps a little tomato sauce or at times with a fried egg on top.

Good Mexican cooks (or good cooks anywhere, for that matter) will tell you not to stir

Beans and rice, two of the staples in Mexican cooking.

rice while it is cooking. If you absolutely have to stir to prevent it from sticking to the bottom of the pan, use a fork. A spoon will tend to mash the grains and, of course, you want to see each cooked grain separate.

In Mexico, they use the long-grain "un-converted" rice usually, though many of us in the United States prefer the "converted" type. At any rate, for best results, please follow cooking directions for each recipe exactly. Even a small amount of overcooking can give you a mush.

Avocados

This is a native fruit, pear shaped and with a rather thick green skin. It was highly prized by the Indians for its smooth, buttery flavor. The pulp, when scooped out, is the basis for that most famous of dips, *guacamole*. Rich in vitamin A, it is both nutritious and flavorful. Many years ago, the parent *aguacate* was transplanted from the state of Puebla to California, where it found a most hospitable soil. It flourished so well, in fact, that it soon began to produce fabulous crops.

Better exercise a little caution when buying avocados, however. Unless you live in an area where you can pick them off nearby trees, never wait to buy them until the day you want to use them. They come to city markets hard and green, and you should plan on letting them ripen in a warm kitchen for three or four days before using. If you are an uncertain shopper, it's a good idea to enlist the cooperation of the storekeeper. Tell him when you want to use the avocados and how many you will need.

The fruit is right for eating when it is just tender. If the pit moves when you shake the fruit or if the skin begins to separate from the flesh, you have probably waited too long, for these are sure signs of old age. Always prepare avocados at the last minute, as they have a tendency to discolor when exposed to air.

Avocado production in California, our major supplier (southern Florida is the only other area to produce any significant crop), is being seriously jeopardized. For the first time since the groves were planted sixty years ago, they are being threatened by a people blight.

A tide of city exiles from the coastal areas of California, trying to escape the pressures of city life, is sweeping the avocado country, and developers are already paying fantastic prices for land. While thousands of acres of new avocado groves have been planted in recent years because of an upsurge in demand, the growers are having their problems. It would be a pity if that pale green, creamy fruit became a scarce luxury.

Plantains

This fruit is commonly used throughout Latin America and the Caribbean area as a vegetable. It is similar to the banana in appearance, except for its green color. In a pinch, you could substitute an unripe banana. The plantain has to be cooked before it is edible, and frequently it is sautéed in lard.

Lard

Lard is the principal cooking fat, which is really not surprising considering the number of pigs being raised. Olive oil and salad oil run equally for second place, but you can substitute vegetable shortening if you prefer. Butter is not used as much as the other fats.

Nuts and Seeds

These are often ground and used for thickening sauces as well as for flavoring. Some cooks use corn flour (*masa harina*) for thickening, but they don't rely on eggs and flour as we do. The Spaniards brought almonds, hazelnuts, walnuts, pine nuts (*pignoli*) and sesame seeds to Mexico, where they grow very well and are well established in the cuisine. The native *cacahuete* (peanut) is often used in sauces to accompany meat.

Cheese

While the Spaniards introduced cheese to Mexico, the Indians quickly learned how to make many of the cheeses for which Spain was famous. Fortunately, the dairy cattle brought by the Spanish did well in their new country, and today cheese making is a thriving industry. Can you imagine tostados or tacos without that sprinkling of grated cheese? While it is difficult to track down Mexican cheese in this country, you can substitute Monterey Jack or even Muenster, which "strings" nicely.

Mozzarella also "strings" well but lacks some of the flavor needed. Buy cheese by the block; it's easier to grate than the ready-sliced and doesn't dry out as quickly.

Fish and Seafood

With its more than 4000 miles of coastline, Mexico produces a tremendous lot of fish and seafood, which are a part of the cuisine. Since there is good airfreight service, good roads and splendid rail routes, fish can be shipped all over the country. In addition to shrimp, lobsters, oysters, crabs, clams, tuna, red snapper, flounder, bass and many others familiar to us, there is also a wide choice of freshwater fish.

If you live a long way inland, away from coastal areas and lakes, you need to be able to judge a fresh fish unless you have absolute, implicit faith in your dealer. The eyes should be bright and not sunken, and the gills a clear, reddish color. The flesh should be firm enough so that when you press it, the fingers don't leave any indentation. It might be simpler if you let your fish dealer know that you completely depend on him for top quality and most likely he'll be happy to oblige.

Meats

The Mexicans are great pork eaters, and most country people keep a couple of pigs in their backyard. In the north, however, more beef is eaten. The cattle feed on wild oregano, which gives the meat an extragood flavor. The Spaniards introduced goats, and young kid, *cabrito*, is very good when the animal is no more than thirty days old. After that, it starts to graze and the flesh develops a strong flavor and becomes tough. The Mexicans, with their usual inventiveness, have developed many ways of preparing delicious meat dishes, from *barbocoa de carnero* (barbecued meat) to meats bathed in the numerous savory *moles* or sauces.

Chorizos

These are sausages, spicy and hot. They play a star role in many dishes and are used as a filling for tortillas and even with scrambled eggs. If you don't live near a Mexican or Spanish store, you can substitute the Italian hot sausage quite handily.

Chocolate

This was one of the surprising delights that captivated Cortés and his men. At that time the cacao bean was so valuable that the Aztecs used it not only as the chief ingredient of their favorite beverage, but also as money for bartering. Certainly it fascinated early European writers, who tell us that it was drunk only by the nobles and by the affluent. Even then, it was used in moderation, for the general idea prevailed that it could cause mental derangement if taken to excess, just as some of the hallucinogenic mushrooms could.

At a later date, so the story goes, the women of Chiapas were so addicted that they took to drinking cups of chocolate while attending church. Perhaps this was to sustain them during an extralong sermon. When the bishop ordered them to stop this habit, they refused to obey and so were excommunicated.

While Mexican chocolate has a lighter body than ours, with a definite texture and flavor of its own (there's a touch of cinnamon), it should not deter us from enjoying this delicious beverage. It's easy to concoct our own with what is available in local stores.

Herbs, Spices and Vanilla

Herbs, spices and other flavorings are very important ingredients, for they give the final, authoritative touch to Mexican cooking. The most popular are within easy reach on our supermarket shelves, so they shouldn't present any problem. From anise and allspice to bay leaf, cinnamon and cloves, ground coriander, marjoram and oregano—we are familiar with all of them. One or two might pose a challenge, such as fresh green coriander or *cilantro,* as the Mexicans call it. It is also known as Chinese parsley. If you live near a specialty store or a Chinese market, you might be lucky enough to find it. Shops that import food from India or Puerto Rico just might have it on hand. If you aren't fortunate enough to locate *cilantro,* we can't honestly suggest a substitute. The nearest approach would be Italian parsley, which resembles it in appearance, but the flavors are not alike.

Epazote: This is an herb that is used in many tortilla dishes. It is very difficult to track down when fresh, but it can be purchased in the dried form. (See page 93 for sources of supply.) Always remember when using dried herbs that they are much more concentrated than the fresh, so use much less.

Achiote or Annatto: This is fairly well distributed in our supermarkets, especially since many of them now have sections specializing in Spanish and Mexican foods. Used both to flavor foods and to color them an appetizing buttercup yellow, it is also popular in England. Its chief use there is to color butter during the winter months when the cows can't get out to pasture and the cream begins to look a bit anemic.

Most of the spices and herbs called for in Mexican dishes are readily available to us. Although Mexico produces as many as thirteen kinds of oregano, for instance, you don't need to be a botanist to "cook Mexican." Just head for the spice shelf at your supermarket.

Vanilla: Top choice among all our luscious flavors, vanilla is a native of Mexico. It enchanted Cortés and the *conquistadores,* who were the first white men to enjoy it.

Used for centuries by the Aztecs, it grew only in Mexico for three hundred years after its discovery by the Spaniards. The product of a special type of orchid, it requires a lot of care to grow and propagate. Today Mexico is a minor supplier of the vanilla bean; the bulk of our imports come from Madagascar.

Picked green, the beans are thoroughly pampered for ten days while they lie on blankets in the sun during the day. Then they spend each night wrapped in their blankets in a warehouse. By this time, they have turned a dark brown and have slimmed to the size of a pencil. So precious are these beans that growers actually brand them with their own identifying mark to prevent "rustlers" from taking them.

There is a charming Mexican legend about the origin of vanilla. Once there was an Aztec general who was sent in search of some fugitive Totonac Indians after they had refused to deliver six maidens as tribute to the Aztec king. All at once he found himself deep in the jungle. There were no maidens in sight, but the air was filled with a marvelous, delicious perfume we now know as vanilla. After tracking down the source, he picked some of the branches and pods, then returned home without the maidens. The king was so delighted with this "find" that he mixed it with his chocolate to produce a beverage that was, well—fit for a king! So from then on, the Totonacs had to pay tribute to the king in vanilla pods, and forget the girls! The Indians called this new-found treasure *tlilxochitl,* meaning "black flower." Small wonder that the Spaniards couldn't pronounce this, so they named it *vainilla,* meaning "little pod." From there it's only a short step to our English name, vanilla.

Some Classic Mexican Dishes at a Glance

Tortillas: Considered the daily bread of Mexico, these flat, wafer-thin pancakes are made of *masa* (cornmeal dough) and browned on a *comal,* a flat skillet usually made of clay. They form the basis of many other dishes and are used by the lower-income groups as plates that are edible, scoops for claiming the last bit of food and for dipping into sauces.

Tacos: For the usual taco, take a freshly baked tortilla, top with cooked, shredded meat smothered in a spicy sauce, and fold in half. Another version is to fry the filled tortilla in hot lard. Turn when one side is brown and quickly fry on the other side. You've already taken the precaution of fastening the opening with a toothpick, which should be removed before serving. Tacos should not be fried too crisp, or, to follow the Mexican rule, *"no deben tronar"*—they mustn't thunder or they will explode.

Enchiladas: Tortillas are fried briefly in hot lard, dipped in a chili sauce, and then wrapped around a sausage and sauce mixture. As a final touch, they are sprinkled with grated cheese and chopped onion.

Burritos: Tortillas made of wheat flour instead of the usual *masa* are rolled up over a savory filling. This may be beans with cheese (Muenster will do nicely) or crumbled, cooked *chorizo* (sausage).

Chalupas: Tortillas with the edges turned up are fried and then covered with meat, beans, chili pepper, tomato and onions.

Gorditas: Translated as "little fat ones," these are tortillas that are smaller and fatter than usual. Generally they are cooked with a variety of chopped meat and vegetables, with cheese, shredded lettuce and chili pepper sauce.

Panuchos: Tortillas are filled with beans, corn, fish or chicken with chili and spices.

Empanadas: These are turnovers made of wheat-flour pastry, filled with meat, fish, or vegetables, then fried in lard. They are not restricted to Mexico and are also very popular in Chile and other South American countries.

Tamales: Made of *masa*, the Mexican corn dough, these are rolled out, filled with beans or meat, and flavored with chili. They are then rolled into a shape like a small banana and steamed in corn husks or banana leaves.

Elote: A great favorite, this is green corn on the cob.

Cebiche: Raw fish or seafood is marinated in lemon or lime juice or vinegar, together with oil, salt, pepper, onion and chili pepper. It is thought that *cebiche* originated with the ancient fishermen of Peru before they became

familiar with the use of fire.

Tingas: This form of stew has an ancestry of Spanish and Mexican foods. Precooked meat such as *chorizo* (sausage) is added to a stock with herbs, spices, onions, chili, garlic and tomatoes.

Moles: These are national sauces made with chilies and many other ingredients. Mexico is a land of sauces, and the most famous of all is the internationally known *mole poblano*. This is the chili sauce from Puebla that contains bitter chocolate among many other ingredients and is served with turkey or chicken, called by the Mexicans *mole de guajalote.*

Quesadillas: These are turnovers of *masa* (corn dough) filled with cheese, potatoes and a variety of meats or fish. They are then fried in hot lard and smothered with grated cheese and sauce.

Torta: This is a sandwich made with a roll sliced in half lengthwise.

Albóndigas: These highly seasoned meat-balls are served fried or in a stew.

Barbacoa de carnero: Barbecued meat, one of the most ancient methods of cooking meat, was popular at the time of the *conquistadores* and dates back for centuries. It is one of the most ancient methods of cooking meat and is still one of the best. A pit is dug in the ground and preheated with a wood fire placed over rocks. The Mexicans then line the pit with maguey spikes, which add a marvelous flavor to the meat. After the whole animal, often lamb or mutton, which may at times be cut up before cooking, is placed in the pit, it is covered with earth and left for about eight hours until it is thoroughly cooked. Direct descendants of this delicious way of preparing meat are the Hawaiian luau and the New England clambake.

Buñuelos: These flaky, fried cakes are made from a wheat-flour dough. Throughout Spain and Latin America you can find many versions of *buñuelos,* some savory, others sweet. In Mexico they may be rolled out until very thin, to as much as twelve inches in diameter; then they are fried crisp and stacked up until ready to serve. Mostly of the sweet type of fritter, they are sometimes broken up and heated in a thick syrup or *piloncillo* (Mexican brown sugar) and occasionally flavored with anise.

Bizcochos, postres and pasteles: The Mexicans have a very sweet tooth, so this variety of cookies, desserts and pastries offers a large array of temptations that are decorative and delicious. The visitor to Mexico will have a difficult time deciding which to choose. *Dulces,* or candies, are for sale everywhere, so the calorie watcher should be warned.

Flan: This caramel custard has found its way around the world. Originating in Spain, it is a tremendous favorite in Mexico, where its smooth, rich flavor is very appealing.

Antojitos: Translated literally as "little whims," *antojitos* are appetizers and snacks. Snacking is one of the favorite pastimes in Mexico, and you have only to walk down the street of any town or village to find an endless variety of foods for nibbling. They range from tortillas stuffed with all kinds of fillings, to clams, pumpkin seeds, peanuts, freshly fried enchiladas and tacos or whatever! At any street corner you are apt to find a woman with her charcoal brazier serving up ears of roasted corn and other tidbits, all with a most tantalizing aroma.

Beverages — Alcoholic and Nonalcoholic

Tequila: With a reputation for being very potent, tequila is distilled from the liquid obtained from the pineapple-shaped base of the maguey plant. The Mexican manner of drinking it is with a little salt and a quarter of a lime. First, they taste the salt, swallow some tequila and then extract the juice from the lime by biting it.

Pulque: This is also from the maguey, but unlike tequila, it is prepared from the milky substance extracted from the center of the plant and then fermented.

Beer: This is an old-time beverage in Mexico. The first license for a brew of barley, lemon, tamarind and sugar was issued in 1544. Mexican beer is famous for its quality and is considered the perfect accompaniment to some of the spicier foods.

Sangría: Borrowed from Spain, this is a blend of red wine with sugar, lemon or lime juice and carbonated water. Mixed in a large glass pitcher, sections of grapefruit, orange and other fruits are often added to make a very refreshing beverage.

Chocolate: Since this beverage has been covered in other sections of the book, it is sufficient to repeat that the cacao bean, which is its base, is a native of Mexico. The chocolate is served hot and foamy with a light cinnamon flavor.

Atole: This is a thin gruel of cooked corn diluted with fruit juice, cream, ground almonds and milk.

Horchata: This delicious and refreshing nonalcoholic drink is made of ground seeds or nuts mixed with water, sugar and lemon juice. It is also very popular in Spain, where the large almond crop makes it a common beverage in restaurants, cafés and roadside stands. The Spaniard enjoys his almond-based *horchata* much as we patronize our soft-drink stands.

It would be difficult to list the large number of fresh fruit drinks available. Anyone who has ever visited the famous Sanborn's in Mexico City will remember with some nostalgia the assortment of delicious drinks blended to order, from watermelon, peach and apricot, to lime, strawberry and so on. A wonderful way to end a round of shopping!

Foods of the Fiestas

Many of the fiestas celebrated in Mexico are closely bound up with religious festivals. The first missionary friars to Mexico regarded some of the pagan Aztec customs with sympathy and understanding, wisely allowing the Indians to retain some of their fiestas and dancing. These were changed only so that they represented homage to a saint rather than a pagan god.

Mexico is a country where festivals have their own foods, much as we have our traditional turkey for Thanksgiving and Christmas, ham at Easter and watermelon for the Fourth of July. A great deal is made of family gatherings in Mexico, for the family is a closely knit unit.

New Year's Day

Supper is the big meal of the day when the

table is set with the finest tablecloth and a centerpiece of choice fruits. Grapes are a "must," for as the bells ring out at midnight to announce the New Year, each person eats twelve of them to ensure good luck during the coming twelve months.

Menus usually include a soup, perhaps with a base of asparagus, fish, cheese or oysters. Roast suckling pig is a popular meat, though the preferred dish is roast turkey. This may be stuffed with an assortment of nuts, fruits, raisins, citron, pepper, herbs, spices, nutmeg and sometimes ground pork with carrots and olives. Served alongside is an assortment of chilies, peppers and fresh pimientos, making the diners' plates a riot of color.

Assorted salads take an important place in the meal. A traditional favorite includes beets, lettuce and boiled potatoes or perhaps it is made up of oranges, limes and pears with an oil and vinegar dressing seasoned with oregano and onion. *Bacalao,* or dried codfish, in tomato sauce also has an important place on the New Year's table. Then, since most Mexicans have a great fondness for sweet foods, the meal ends with *postres* and *dulces* (desserts and candies). There may be *turrones* (sugared almond nougat), coconut candy, *flan* (caramel custard) and the ever popular *buñuelos* (fried flaky pastry drenched with a syrup).

Rosca de Reyes

Rosca refers to a ring-shaped cake of yeast dough combined with sugar, eggs, orange-flower water, grated lemon rind and butter. This is served on January 6 (Twelfth Night) to celebrate the arrival of the Three Kings (*Reyes)* in Bethlehem as they carried gifts for the Christ child. A small figure of a child, usually of porcelain, is hidden in the dough of the *rosca,* and the person finding it is expected to give a party on February 2 for everyone present. This is the day when the infant figure is removed from the crèche and put away until the following year.

Lent and Holy Week

For a people as dedicated to good food as the Mexicans, this time of year brings a drastic change in eating habits. Fish and seafood generally replace meat, and meals become simpler. Some of the usual Lenten meals consist of soup, pasta (macaroni, spaghetti, etc.), *empanadas* filled with vegetables or seafood, *bacalao* (dried codfish), shrimp or tuna with a spicy sauce, salad and a classical dessert of bread fried in oil with brown sugar, cheese, cinnamon, raisins and peanuts. While this sounds as though the Mexicans are not exactly deprived during Lent, they are giving up many of their favorite meat and poultry dishes.

Dia de Muertos or Day of the Dead

This day falls on November 2, corresponding to All Souls' Day in other Catholic as well as Protestant countries. If the Day of the Dead in Mexico sounds mournful, it isn't a bit! The history of this holiday goes back to the days of the missionary friars in 1562. Since the Indians already had a festival to venerate the dead about this time of year, it was fairly simple to guide them into the Christian ritual.

The whole atmosphere is one of gaiety in the busy days beforehand as favorite foods of the departed are prepared. At this time, shops are filled with beautifully made creations of small figures, skulls, skeletons and other symbols of death, all made of sugar. The Mexicans see nothing incongruous in licking the rounded top of a sugar skull. Foods to celebrate the occasion may include *alfajor* (a coconut paste with honey and nuts), peanuts, caramel, anise and jellied pastes of guava, peach and quince. There may also be pumpkin baked in honey, almond paste, different kinds of tamales, stuffed peppers and a variety of "breads of the dead." These breads are made with a feather-light yeast dough, delicately flavored and topped with dough shaped like crossed bones, all of it heavily sprinkled with sugar. Many Mexicans visit the cemeteries that day, and a large number eat their offerings to the dead while sitting on the gravestones to chat with friends and neighbors.

Posadas and Christmas

This is another example of the blending of Christian and Aztec rites. Since Christmas coincided with the Aztec celebrations honoring one of their gods, Huitzilopochtli, the friars preserved some of the original fiestas, changing them enough to give them a Christian character.

Posada is the Spanish word for an inn or lodging house, and no doubt when the Mexicans refer to the *posadas*, they have in mind the search for lodgings in Bethlehem by the Holy Family. These celebrations take place between December 16 and 24, and for each of these nine nights, the wanderings of Mary and Joseph as they search for lodging are re-enacted in every *posada*.

Dressed as pilgrims, the people form processions, carrying beautifully carved figures depicting scenes in the life of Jesus. Often they carry lighted candles as they go from door to door, singing their request for lodging. The host sings his refusal, but when he finally opens the door, everyone crowds in to spend the rest of the evening there. Part of the fun includes the blindfolding of one of the children whose task it is to find the *piñata* hanging from the ceiling. The *piñata* is a traditional container made of gaily colored earthenware or paper and filled with candy, fruit and other goodies. When the *piñata* is finally broken, there is a mad scramble for all the *dulces* and fruits. After this, gifts are exchanged, and then the serious business of eating commences. Christmas dinner is very similar to that served on New Year's with stuffed turkey as the star attraction, followed by numerous salads and desserts, making it one of the gargantuan meals of the year.

A statue of Quetzalcoatl, the lengendary plumed serpent.

Mexican Mealtimes

The *desayuno* (breakfast) starts the day. In the cities it tends to be rather light, consisting of sweet rolls and coffee or hot chocolate. In the country, however, it is often more substantial and may include eggs and even steak if the family is affluent enough.

The *comida* or dinner is the big meal of the day and is usually served anywhere from noon to 5:00 P.M. Because of the high altitude (Mexico City is 7,500 feet above sea level), most Mexican prefer to eat lightly in the evening. The *comida* may consist of as many as seven courses, beginning with an appetizer. This is followed by a traditional soup and then by what is known as "dry" soup, not really a soup at all but a pasta dish or perhaps rice. Fish may be next, then a main course of poultry or meat, accompanied by salad and vegetables. The last course is the *postre,* or dessert, and the meal ends with coffee or tea.

A *merienda,* or snack, generally falls due about 6:00 P.M., a time for coffee or hot chocolate with cakes, cookies or pastries. Another *merienda* is often enjoyed sometime between 8:00 and 10:00 P.M. Both the Mexicans and the Spanish are great "snackers," and this frequent nibbling enables them to go for rather long periods between regular mealtimes.

Cena, which is actually translated as "dinner," usually refers to a gala meal for a special occasion with guests. This may take place in Mexico any time between 10:00 P.M. and midnight.

The most popular and best-known of all Mexican appetizers—guacamole.

1
Appetizers

While the North Americans can claim the introduction of the *coctel* or cocktail party, the Mexican hostess has added her own special touch to the appetizers. There may very well be the familiar dish of salted peanuts, since these are native to Mexico, but the guest will also savor many of the foods used for *meriendas,* or snacks. So it is very possible to enjoy tortillas stuffed with a savory filling, *empanadas* (pastry turnovers) and canapes using small tostados spread with savory refried beans. All of these are served in miniature portions with deference to the *cena,* or gala meal, ahead.

Guacamole I

The most famous of all the appetizer spreads, it is a favorite "dip" of the American hostess.

1 large, ripe avocado	1 small *serrano* (hot chili), chopped,
2 Tbs. fresh lime juice	*or* 1 teaspoon chili powder
½ cup finely chopped, peeled tomato	Dash of paprika
1 tsp. salt	⅛ tsp. pepper
2 tsp. finely chopped onion	Pinch of cayenne pepper

Peel and mash avocado with a fork. Blend in remaining ingredients. To make ahead of time, put the pit in the spread (remove before serving) and cover tightly with foil or plastic wrap.

Makes approximately 1½ cups.

Guacamole II

A blender is useful here but not necessary.

1 medium tomato *or* ¼ cup canned	1½ Tbs. lemon juice
tomatoes, drained	1 tsp. salt
1 tsp. chili powder	⅛ tsp. pepper
¼ cup finely chopped onion	2 ripe avocados

If using fresh tomato, dip in boiling water for 1 minute, then in cold water. The skin should then peel off easily with a small knife. Blend in chili powder, chopped onion, lemon juice, salt and pepper.

Peel avocados, cut in half and remove pit. Mash with a fork or place in blender with other ingredients. After all ingredients are well mixed, place in covered container and chill before serving.

Makes 1½ cups, approximately.

Tip: A ripe avocado feels soft and not too firm to the touch. There should be no blemishes on the skin. When buying, don't press hard or you will bruise the fruit and make yourself very unpopular with the merchant. A better idea is to let the merchant pick out the fruit for you and tell him just when you want to use it. Always peel avocados just before using, for they discolor quickly when exposed to the air.

Chile con Queso para Sopar
Chili and Cheese Dip

Even though we think of a cocktail spread as "fun food," it can also be nutritious. The cheese in this recipe not only adds flavor but contributes valuable protein and calcium.

1 Tbs. finely chopped onion
1 clove garlic, crushed
2 Tbs. olive oil
1 cup solid-pack tomatoes
1 can (4 oz.) peeled green chilies, chopped
2 slices bacon, crisply cooked
½ lb. Monterey Jack cheese, shredded
1 cup light cream
Salt and pepper to taste

Combine onion and garlic and add to olive oil. Add tomatoes and place mixture in a small saucepan. Bring to a boil, then reduce heat and stir constantly over moderate heat for 2 or 3 minutes. Add chopped chilies. Crumble bacon and add. Stir in cheese. As the cheese begins to melt, add cream, salt and pepper. Turn into a heated dish and serve hot with *tostaditos* or corn chips. A chafing dish is ideal for serving.

Makes approximately 3 cups.

Frijoles para Sopar
Bean Dip

"Someday some historical bone-picker seeking a subject for a world-shaking thesis that will live as long as Shakespeare, will hit upon the lowly bean. What a welter of knowledge he will develop in his research and I am sure he will come to the conclusion that without the bean, the earth would have long since slipped into orbit and disappeared among a galaxy inhabited by bean-eaters. Hail to the bean!" So wrote the late Senator Everett M. Dirksen in this paean of praise to the bean.

The Mexicans have shown us that the bean can take on glamour when served with a little imagination.

1 can (8 oz.) red kidney beans
2 slices bacon
1 Tbs. finely chopped scallion
1 Tbs. chopped green bell pepper
1 clove garlic, minced
¼ tsp. salt
½ tsp. chili powder
¼ tsp. monosodium glutamate (Accent)
1 cup dairy sour cream
Pepper to taste
Pinch of cayenne pepper

Clockwise from top left: corn chips, chili and cheese dip, guacamole and bean dip.

Drain and mash kidney beans. Fry bacon crisp and reserve. Add bacon fat slowly to kidney beans and stir over low heat until all fat is absorbed. Combine chopped scallions with chopped bell pepper, garlic, salt, chili powder, monosodium glutamate and sour cream. Crumble bacon and add to sour cream mixture. Stir into beans. Add pepper and cayenne pepper and blend well. Serve with *tostaditos* or corn chips.

Makes 2 cups.

Coctel de Camarones
Shrimp Cocktail

If you absolutely despise shelling shrimp, you can use the canned variety for this dish, but the fresh ones taste much, much better. Shell and devein about 1 pound of shrimp in the usual manner *after* cooking. You get more flavor that way. The best way to cook them for a cocktail is to simmer in water with a bay leaf and peppercorns for a few minutes until they turn pink. Don't overcook. Marinate in the sauce, refrigerated, for 4 or 5 hours, then serve in cocktail glasses. Or if you prefer, you can serve the shrimp on a platter with the sauce in the center and plenty of toothpicks for the dunkers.

Sauce

3 Tbs. prepared hot mustard	2 Tbs. toasted sesame seeds or pine nuts
¾ cup olive oil	
½ cup white vinegar or lemon juice	Salt and freshly ground pepper to taste

Blend all ingredients and serve chilled. Sesame seeds or pine nuts can be toasted by placing in a shallow pan in a moderate (350°F.) oven for a few minutes, shaking occasionally.

Cebiche
Pickled Fish

Cebiche is a very popular dish in Mexico that can be used as an appetizer or as a light luncheon dish when served in larger portions. If anyone pales at the thought of eating raw fish, they can take comfort in the fact that it is "cooked" by the lemon juice and has been enjoyed by the Indians for centuries.

1 lb. haddock, pompano or whitefish	¼ cup salad oil
	1 Tbs. water
1 cup lemon juice (about 5 lemons)	1 tsp. oregano
	1 tsp. basil
1 can (8 oz.) tomatoes	1 tsp. ground coriander
3 or 4 small hot chilies (*jalapeños* or *serranos*), canned	Salt and pepper to taste

Wash and skin the filleted fish, and cut up into small squares. Place in a glass (not metal) dish and pour lemon juice over. Refrigerate 3 or 4 hours, turning occasionally with a wooden spoon, taking care not to break the fish. Add remaining ingredients and blend carefully. Chill several hours and serve very cold in chilled seafood cocktail glasses. May be garnished with avocado slices and onion rings.

Makes 6 servings.

Empanadas
Baked Turnovers

The English might claim the *empanada* as a Cornish pasty, for it is similar to the lunchbox "special" of Cornish workers. Wives sealed cooked potatoes, vegetables and meat into a pastry crust and so tucked a whole course into a compact package.

Empanadas are popular in South America, especially Chile, and Mexico has adopted them with enthusiasm. You can vary the filling as you wish.

Use half the recipe for pastry on page 24.

Filling

3 Tbs. lard	4 hard-cooked eggs, chopped
2 Tbs. oil	
3 medium onions, chopped	Salt and pepper to taste
1 cup grated Swiss or American cheese	French dressing, if necessary
3 canned pimientos, chopped	

Heat lard and oil in a large skillet and add chopped onion. Stir over moderate heat until onion is tender, not brown. Blend with remaining ingredients and correct seasoning. If mixture seems too dry, moisten with a little French dressing.

Roll out pastry about ⅛ inch thick on lightly floured board and cut in 4-inch squares. Place a rounded tablespoon of filling in the center of each square and fold over to form a triangle. Seal edges well and pierce the top of each with a fork. Place on ungreased cookie sheet and bake in a preheated hot oven (400°F.) for about 25 minutes or until light brown. Serve hot.

Makes approximately 20 *empanadas*.

Pastelillos
Meat Turnovers

First cousin to the *empanada*, these spicy meatballs in pastry will do double duty both as a main dish for luncheon or as an appetizer when fried bite size. Just be sure they are piping hot when you serve them.

2 strips bacon	1 Tbs. chopped onion
1 lb. ground lean beef	1 tsp. oregano
1 can (4½ oz.) ham spread	1 tsp. salt
1 tomato, diced	1 clove garlic, minced
⅓ cup chopped green olives	¼ tsp. black pepper
1 Tbs. capers	2 hard-cooked eggs, chopped

In a large skillet, fry bacon until crisp. Drain and crumble; set aside. Pour off all but 1 teaspoon bacon fat in skillet. Add beef and cook until brown. Stir in ham spread, tomato, olives, capers, chopped onion, oregano, salt, garlic and pepper. Cook over moderate heat, stirring constantly, for 10 minutes. Blend in chopped eggs. Chill for several hours.

Divide pastry into 4 parts. On a lightly floured board, roll each part noodle thin (about ⅛ inch thick). Cut into 3-inch circles. Place 1 rounded teaspoon of meat filling on each circle. Fold dough over to form a half moon and pinch edges together. Crimp with a fork and pierce the top of each. Repeat, using remaining

dough. Fry in deep fat at 375°F. about 3 minutes or until golden. Drain and serve hot. If desired, roll into 6-inch circles with 2 tablespoons of filling on each. Fold over and follow procedure for small turnovers.

Yield: 9 to 10 dozen small turnovers; 4 to 5 dozen large turnovers.

Pastry

6 cups all-purpose flour	½ cup butter
1 Tbs. salt	2 eggs
½ cup lard	1½ cups (approximately) ice water

Sift flour with salt. Rub in lard until mixture forms lumps about the size of peas. Then rub in butter (chilled) until the mixture has the texture of cornmeal. Beat eggs with water and trickle mixture slowly, about 3 tablespoons at a time, down the side of the bowl. Blend with a fork until a small ball of dough is formed. Remove dough and place on a piece of waxed paper. Continue until all mixture is used. Form dough into 1 large ball, wrap in waxed paper and chill for at least 1 hour before rolling out. The secret of good pastry is to keep all the ingredients cold and avoid overworking them.

Carnitas
Little Meats

Here are bites of crisp, juicy pork served hot with all the natural flavor of the meat. Serve with corn chips or any of the snack-type crackers, along with plenty of toothpicks for spearing. This is a very accommodating dish, good for a buffet supper or as a filling for tacos.

2 lbs. lean pork (boneless butt)	Salt and black pepper to taste
¼ tsp. monosodium glutamate (Accent)	

Cut the pork in 1-inch cubes and sprinkle with monosodium glutamate, salt and pepper. Place in a shallow baking pan and bake in a slow oven (300°F.) about 2 hours, pouring off any excess fat from time to time. Serve hot.

Makes 6 to 8 servings.

Tacos con Hongos
Tacos with Mushrooms

This is not the kind of snack you'd find on any street corner. Perhaps you enjoy thinly sliced raw mushrooms in a tossed salad; you'll find them just as delightful in this filling for tacos. You can find canned tortillas in the supermarket, or if you prefer to make your own, see page 35 for the recipe.

½ lb. fresh mush-
  rooms
1 medium onion,
  chopped
2 canned green
  chilies, chopped
1 cup finely shredded
  lettuce

2 large tomatoes,
  skinned and
  chopped
1 tsp. chili powder
Salt and pepper to
  taste
Tomato sauce
12 tortillas
¼ cup hot lard

Thinly slice raw mushrooms and toss with onion, chopped chilies, lettuce, tomatoes, chili powder, salt and pepper. Moisten with a little tomato sauce. Dip the tortillas in hot lard long enough to become limp, then remove with tongs. Divide filling onto tortillas and fold over like a small sandwich.

Makes 12 tacos.

Nachos
An Appetizer

Along with chili con carne, *nachos* are a favorite food just north of the border. Not strictly Mexican but much appreciated by Texans, they come under the heading of Tex-Mex food. *Nachos* are often served as an appetizer with ice cold beer.

Tortillas
Salad oil
Refried beans
Grated Cheddar
  cheese

Pickled *jalapeño*
  peppers, sliced,
  seeds removed

Cut tortillas into quarters. Pour oil in a layer about ¼-inch deep in large skillet, and heat. Fry tortilla pieces in hot oil until golden brown and crisp. Drain on paper towels. Spread with refried beans, sprinkle with grated cheese and top with sliced *jalapeño* peppers. Broil until cheese melts and serve hot.

Pambacitos
Miniature Stuffed Rolls

On many a street the passerby will be tempted by the aroma of roasting corn from a food stand, the *antojitos* ("little whims") such as tortillas, tacos and tostados, along with several other tantalizing morsels.

Compared with the hero-sized *torta,* the *pambacito* is a miniature roll. It's big enough, however, to hold 5 or 6 layers of savories, making it a fairly substantial snack.

1 Tbs. lard
3 *chorizos* (Spanish
  or Italian hot
  sausages)
2 large potatoes,
  freshly boiled and
  diced
1 large onion, finely
  chopped
Salt and pepper to
  taste
1 large egg, lightly
  beaten
12 rolls

Finely shredded
  lettuce
¼ cup French
  dressing
1 cup refried beans
  or canned red
  kidney beans,
  mashed
Tomato sauce
Grated Parmesan
  cheese
12 radishes, thinly
  sliced

Heat lard in a large skillet. Skin and chop sausages and stir over moderate heat for 5 minutes. Add cooked, diced potatoes and chopped onion. Continue stirring until onions are just tender, not brown. Season with salt and pepper. Stir in the lightly beaten egg and cook until egg has set. Keep mixture warm. Add 2 or 3 more tablespoons of lard to skillet. Cut tops off the rolls and set aside. Scoop out all the soft part from the bottom of each roll (save for poultry stuffing or other use) and fry both parts of each roll in the hot lard. Toss the shredded lettuce in French dressing and place a layer in the bottom part of each roll. Cover with a layer of beans, then the sausage mixture, a spoonful or two of tomato sauce, a sprinkling of grated cheese and top with a layer of thinly sliced radish. Replace the top and serve while hot.

Makes 12 *pambacitos.*

Tortas Compuestas
Mexican Sandwiches
Don't wait for *mañana* to fix these Mexican hero sandwiches. They're stacked with cold cuts and avocado slices, sprinkled with chili powder and a dash of garlic powder. Great!

2
Soups: "Wet" and "Dry"

No matter how hot and humid a section of Mexico may be, there is always soup on the menu. Because poultry is plentiful, chicken broth is a favorite. It may be served with perhaps a spoonful of rice in the bottom of the bowl and with lots of shredded chicken. Mexico has regional specialties, just as with other dishes, such as the cheese soup of Sonora or the vegetable broth from the outskirts of Mexico City.

Some of the lesser-known soups are equally outstanding, and many of them make good use of the plentiful fresh vegetables, such as lima beans, corn and squash.

Caldo de Pollo
Chicken Broth

While you could use canned chicken broth for this, you will get an infinitely better flavor if you make your own. Simmer a fowl with its giblets in enough water to cover, with a medium onion, cut up, 2 cloves garlic, 2 bay leaves, a carrot, some celery tops and salt and pepper. Don't let the liquid boil; it toughens the meat. When the fowl is tender, let it cool in the broth, then remove the skin and bones. Shred some of the meat for garnish and use the rest for chicken pie or salad. Now simmer the broth, uncovered, until it is reduced in quantity and the flavor is just right for your taste. Strain before using. Serve very hot with a little cooked rice in the bottom of each bowl and perhaps a few sliced, sautéed mushrooms floating on top.

Sopa de Elote
Corn Soup

Corn, unlike other cereals, is attached to a cob, and for this recipe the kernels must be removed. Don't be tempted to open a can. It's much simpler than scraping corn cobs, but the final result is well worth the extra bit of effort.

6 ears fresh corn	Freshly ground black pepper
2 quarts chicken stock	½ cup heavy cream
½ cup finely chopped onion	1 clove garlic, minced

2 Tbs. butter
⅓ cup tomato puree
2½ tsp. salt
¼ tsp. cayenne pepper
½ tsp. ground cumin

Remove husks from corn and boil 3 of the ears in boiling water to cover for 5 minutes. Remove from water and let cool. Cut kernels off the cob and reserve for later use. Cut kernels from the ears of uncooked corn by first running a small sharp knife down each row of kernels, cutting them in half. Then cut a layer from the entire cob of each. Scrape the cobs with the bowl of a tablespoon. Add to chicken stock with onion, tomato puree, salt and pepper and the reserved cooked corn kernels. Cover and cook slowly for 20 minutes or until raw corn is tender. Add cream and remaining ingredients and cook only until hot. Do not allow to boil or cream may curdle.

Makes 8 servings.

Sopa de Habas con Condimentos
Lima Bean Soup with Condiment Tray

Although lima beans originated in South America, they took to the Mexican soil with enthusiasm and crops are plentiful. The coastal regions of southern California, however, grow more of these beans than any other part of the world.

2 cups fresh baby lima beans or 1 package (10 oz.) frozen baby limas
Water
1 tsp. oregano
1 tsp. salt

Freshly ground black pepper
1 can condensed chicken soup (undiluted)
Bean liquid plus water to fill 1 can
Paprika

For fresh beans, bring 1 cup water to a boil. Add salt, oregano, pepper and beans. If using frozen beans, follow label directions. Boil until tender. Drain and reserve liquid. Either press beans through a fine sieve or use an electric blender and puree them with the liquid you have reserved. Combine with chicken soup and enough water to bring mixture to the consistency you prefer. Reheat and serve in soup bowls. Sprinkle with a little paprika and serve with the following condiments.

Makes 4 to 6 servings.

Condiments

Minced onion
Broken tortillas
Minced green pepper
Sliced green olives
Shredded sharp cheese
Slivered toasted almonds
Sieved hard-cooked egg

Sopa de Garbanzos
Chick Pea Soup

If you have cooked a beef tongue or a ham in the last day or so, here is a savory way of using some of that cooking liquid you hate to throw out. You can substitute dried *garbanzos* for the canned variety if you prefer, but cooking time will be much longer.

4 medium potatoes, peeled and finely diced
1 medium onion, finely chopped
1 clove garlic, minced
2 quarts (8 cups) beef tongue or ham stock

2 cans (1 lb. each) *garbanzos,* or chick peas
1 tsp. salt
Freshly ground black pepper
Pinch cayenne pepper
½ lb. garlic sausage

Add diced potato, onion and garlic to stock and bring to a boil. Simmer until potatoes are just tender. Add chick peas, salt and pepper and reheat. Meantime, pierce sausage with a fork, place in saucepan and cover with cold water. Bring to a boil, then reduce heat to simmer and cook 20 minutes. Add a pinch of cayenne pepper to soup and slice sausage. Add to soup before serving.

Makes 6 to 8 servings.

Sopa de Aguacate
Avocado Soup

It is important to select good avocados to give this soup the rich flavor it should have. If you don't have any tortillas on hand for garnish, you can substitute corn chips. This soup is equally good served ice cold on a hot summer day. Just be sure your chicken stock is free of fat. A couple of drops of green food coloring added at the last minute will give eye appeal.

6 cups chicken broth
Fried tortilla squares
  or corn chips
2 ripe avocados

Heat 1 cup broth and place in electric blender with pulp of one avocado. Blend to a smooth puree and then gradually add pulp of remaining avocado. Add this puree to the remaining 5 cups of broth and heat gently. Do not allow to boil. Correct the seasoning, as it may need salt and perhaps a dash of cayenne pepper. Garnish with fried tortilla squares or corn chips.

Makes 6 to 8 servings.

Sopa de Albóndigas
Meatball Soup

This is a popular item on many restaurant menus. A Mexican might enjoy it with the *comida,* the big meal of the day, but the average American will find it a substantial luncheon dish. Follow with a tossed salad and fresh fruit and you have a complete luncheon.

2 slices white bread
Milk
½ lb. ground sausage
  meat
½ lb. ground veal
½ lb. ground lamb
1 medium onion,
  finely chopped
2 eggs, lightly
  beaten
1½ tsp. salt
Freshly ground
  pepper
2 quarts beef stock
1 cup tomato puree

Soak bread in milk and squeeze dry just before using. Blend meats, onion, eggs and seasonings with bread and mix well. Form into bite-sized balls. Add meatballs to stock that has been blended with tomato puree. Place over moderate heat but do not allow liquid to boil or meatballs will tend to break up. Simmer, covered, for 1 hour, or until meatballs are thoroughly cooked through.

Makes 8 servings.

Caldo de Queso
Cheese Soup

Like many Mexican soups, this is fairly substantial. Follow with an omelet, a small salad and a light dessert, and you have a good luncheon menu.

3 medium potatoes,
   peeled and cut in
   1-inch cubes
5 cups beef broth
2 Tbs. peanut oil
1 small onion, sliced
1 clove garlic, minced
1 lb. tomatoes,
   .chopped, *or* 1 can
   (1 lb.) tomatoes
1 canned *serrano*
   chili, cut in strips
1 sprig dried *epazote*
   (optional)
1 tsp. salt
6 thin slices mild
   American cheese

Add cubed potatoes to broth and bring to a boil. Cook, covered, over moderate heat until potatoes are just tender, about 10 minutes. Heat oil in skillet. Add onion and garlic and stir over moderate heat until onion is tender but not brown. Add fresh or canned tomatoes and stir 10 minutes over moderate heat until mixture has thickened a little. Add to potato-broth mixture. Remove seeds from chili and cut in strips. Add to broth mixture with *epazote*, if used, and stir over moderate heat 5 minutes. It may be necessary to adjust the seasoning at this point, but remember that the cheese contains some salt. Add cheese to hot soup and serve as cheese is melting.

Makes 8 servings.

Sopas Secas (Dry Soups)

Nobody knows why these dishes are called dry soups in Mexico, for they really aren't soups at all. About all we know is that they follow the regular soup in a traditional Mexican meal and are frequently servings of cooked rice with other ingredients or pasta, such as vermicelli with sausage.

One theory for this strange misnomer is that the Spaniards put both rice and pasta into soup and the Aztecs may have considered this a postscript to the wet soup, leading to the distinction between wet and dry soup. We'll never know!

Arroz a la Mexicana
Rice Mexican Style

Depending on the type of rice you use, measure the amount of stock or liquid called for in label directions. "Converted" rice uses a different amount of liquid than the regular long-grain type, and it is important to measure correctly. Otherwise, you may end up with mush or, even worse, rice that is burned dry.

1 cup rice
1 large onion,
   chopped
3 cloves garlic
4 to 4½ cups beef
   stock, fresh or
   canned
¼ cup salad oil
1½ cups canned plum
   tomatoes
Salt and pepper to
   taste
1 cup cooked peas,
   fresh or frozen
1 avocado, peeled
   and sliced

Wash rice if necessary. Place onion and garlic in blender with ½ cup stock. Blend until smooth. Heat oil in skillet and sauté rice until golden. Place rice in saucepan and add onion puree and tomatoes, remaining stock, salt and pepper. Bring to a boil, cover and cook until rice is just tender. Stir in peas until heated through. Garnish with avocado slices.

Makes 6 servings.

Sopa Seca de Fideos con Chorizos
Dry Soup with Vermicelli and
Spanish Sausage

This dry soup makes an interesting alternative to the usual potato or other starchy food in the dinner menu. It would pair attractively either with creamed spinach or sautéed zuchini slices.

3 Tbs. lard or oil
2 Spanish or
   Italian hot
   sausages
1 package (8 oz.)
   vermicelli or thin
   noodles
1 medium onion,
   chopped
2 cloves garlic
1 can (1 lb.) to-
   matoes
1 tsp. oregano
Salt and pepper to
   taste
½ tsp. sugar
1½ cups beef or
   chicken stock
¼ cup grated
   Parmesan cheese
Additional grated
   cheese to serve
   separately

Heat 2 tablespoons lard or oil in large skillet. Skin and chop sausages and cook in hot fat until brown. Remove with slotted spoon and drain on paper towels. Add remaining tablespoon of lard or oil to skillet and add noodles. Cook, stirring constantly, over moderate heat until golden brown. Drain and place in lightly oiled 3-quart casserole. Place onion, garlic and tomatoes in blender and blend until smooth. Reheat fat in skillet, adding a little more lard or oil if necessary. Add tomato mixture and stir over moderate heat for 5 minutes. Blend in oregano, salt, pepper and sugar together with stock. Pour over noodles in casserole and cover with a layer of the cooked sausage. Bake, uncovered, in a moderate (350°F.) oven about 30 minutes or until noodles are tender and all liquid is absorbed. Sprinkle with grated cheese just before serving and serve with additional cheese on the side.

Makes 6 servings.

Sopa Seca de Tortillas
Tortilla Dry Soup

If you don't want to make tortillas specially for this *sopa seca*, look for the canned variety on the supermarket shelves. You'll get better results if you open the can the day before using. Give homemade tortillas a day to dry out a little.

6 green bell peppers	Salt and pepper to taste
½ cup salad oil	¼ tsp. sugar
1 medium onion, finely chopped	1½ dozen small day-old tortillas
1 clove garlic, minced	1 cup (½ pint) heavy cream
2 tablespoons butter	1 cup (¼ lb.) grated Parmesan cheese

Wash and dry green peppers. Place in a shallow pan under broiler about 5 to 6 inches from source of heat, and broil until skin blisters. Place in a brown paper bag with top twisted to close it and leave for 15 minutes. Then run cold water over peppers and skin will come off easily. Remove seeds and coarsely chop peppers. Heat oil in heavy skillet and sauté onion and garlic until tender but not brown. Add chopped green peppers and stir over moderate heat until soft. Season with salt, pepper and sugar, and mix well. Remove mixture with a slotted spoon and drain on paper towels. Cut tortillas in ½-inch strips and sauté in hot fat but do not let them get crisp and brown. Drain on paper towels. Lightly grease a 2-quart casserole and place tortillas in. Pour cream over. Cover with green pepper mixture, then top with a layer of grated cheese. Dot with butter and bake in a moderate (350°F.) oven about 30 minutes until mixture is hot and cheese melted.

Makes 6 servings.

Sopa de Calabaza
Squash Soup, Mexican Style

1 lb. summer squash	
1½ quarts (6 cups) chicken stock	½ tsp. ground black pepper
½ cup diced fresh onion	Dash red pepper
1 tsp. salt	2 egg yolks
¼ cup butter	½ cup heavy cream
2 Tbs. flour	¼ cup crumbled crackers
	Ground nutmeg

Wash and slice squash (do not peel). Place in a saucepan with 3 cups of the stock, onion and salt. Cover and cook 10 minutes or until squash falls apart. Pour by small amounts into food blender. Add remaining stock and blend. Melt butter in large saucepan. Blend flour into melted butter until it begins to brown. Gradually add squash and stock mixture into butter-flour mixture along with black pepper and red pepper. Cook until the soup is slightly thickened, 5 to 7 minutes. Blend egg yolks with cream and crackers and stir into hot soup. Serve hot, each serving garnished with a dash of nutmeg.

Makes 6 servings, 1 cup each.

Eggs 3

Mexican cooking is made up, primarily, of hearty, highly-flavored dishes that are low in cost and very adaptable. Success does not hang on your being able to exactly follow intricate instructions, and you will find that ingredients can often be adjusted to suit your taste (or what you have on hand) without impairing the quality of the finished dish. Like all good peasant fare, the distinctive flavor of Mexican cooking depends on the imaginative use of available ingredients. Simple dishes are transformed, through the use of new, "exotic" seasonings, into star attractions. Here are hearty egg dishes substantial enough to serve as the main course at a brunch or luncheon, or as a delicious, easy-to-fix late supper after the theater. A crisp salad and fresh fruit complete the meal.

Huevos Rancheros
Eggs Country Style

The Spaniards introduced the domestic hen to Mexico, but Mexicans then created their own special egg dishes. *Huevos Rancheros* is a classic and can be found on nearly every restaurant menu in the country.

3 Tbs. lard	1 cup refried beans (page 65) *or* mashed canned kidney beans
12 small (4-inch) tortillas	
12 eggs (2 per person)	1 can (5 oz.) *chilies serranos* (optional)
1 cup tomato sauce	

Heat lard in skillet and fry tortillas, 2 or 3 at a time, until cooked to taste, either limp or crisp. Drain on paper towels and place 2 on each of 6 heated plates. Keep warm. Fry eggs in skillet, adding more lard if necessary. Place a fried egg on each tortilla and spoon hot tomato sauce over it. Serve with refried beans or mashed canned beans on the side with *serrano* chilies.

Makes 6 servings.

Huevos Revueltos
Scrambled Eggs

There's nothing very new about these scrambled eggs except the flavor! You can serve them on toast if you wish or make them more festive by surrounding them with a ring of rice that has been cooked in chicken broth instead of water.

6 large eggs
3 Tbs. lard
1 Tbs. finely minced onion
1 tsp. minced parsley

1 large ripe tomato, chopped
1 tsp. chili powder
Salt and pepper to taste

Beat eggs lightly with a fork. Melt lard in skillet and, when hot, add minced onion. Cook until limp, then add parsley, chopped tomato and chili powder. Cook for 2 or 3 minutes over moderate heat, stirring constantly. Then add beaten eggs and continue to stir over low to moderate heat until eggs are just cooked.

Makes 6 servings.

Huevos Chapultepec
Eggs Chapultepec

The emperor Maximilian lived in Chapultepec during his brief reign in the 1860s. Probably he never enjoyed this dish named after his palace, but fortunately we can.

6 thin slices Muenster or Swiss Cheese
¾ cup diced cooked ham or tongue
6 large eggs
½ cup minced dill pickles

6 Tbs. tomato sauce
1 tsp. chili powder
Salt and pepper to taste
3 Tbs. butter

Lightly grease a shallow baking dish, about 8×8 or 9×9 inches. Place slices of cheese in dish. Blend diced ham or tongue with minced pickles and sprinkle over cheese slices. Break an egg onto each cheese slice. Blend tomato sauce and chili powder and pour over eggs. Sprinkle with salt and pepper to taste. Dot with butter and bake in a preheated, moderate (350°F.) oven just until whites are set but yolks stiff soft, about 10 to 15 minutes.

Makes 6 servings.

Huevos con Camarones
Eggs with Shrimp

This makes a satisfying luncheon or supper dish when served with a tossed salad and a light dessert.

2 Tbs. oil
2 Tbs. lard
1 large onion, finely chopped

½ lb. fresh shrimp, shelled, deveined and coarsely chopped

2 cloves garlic, minced
2 medium tomatoes, chopped, *or* 1 cup canned plum tomatoes, drained
3 canned *jalapeño* chilies, rinsed and seeded, *or* 1 green bell pepper, cut in strips and sautéed

Salt to taste
Freshly ground black pepper
6 large eggs
1 lemon, cut in wedges

Heat oil and lard in heavy skillet. Sauté onion and garlic. If green bell pepper is used, add to onion mixture and stir over moderate heat until both onion and pepper strips are tender. Add chopped tomatoes, fresh or canned, and cook 5 minutes, stirring occasionally. If using chilies, add at this point, together with chopped shrimp, salt and pepper. Remove from heat. Beat eggs with a fork until well blended, then scramble into shrimp mixture over moderately low heat. Stir constantly with a wooden spoon to reach entire surface of pan. To make sure you aren't leaving any areas to scorch, stir from the center of the pan outward in concentric circles until you reach the edge; then repeat. Eggs will set to a creamy consistency in 3 or 4 minutes. Then cook 1 more minute *without stirring* to let mixture set. Cut in pie-shaped servings and garnish with lemon wedges.

Makes 4 to 6 servings.

Huevos a la Malagueña
Eggs Malaga Style

This is a colorful, attractive dish that can be put together in very little time. An oval oven-to-table platter would be ideal for use here. Since you already have three vegetables in the recipe, you may want to serve a fruit or gelatin salad with ice cream and cookies to follow.

4 Tbs. butter
4 slices boiled ham
1 can (15 oz.) asparagus
4 thick slices tomato
1 can (6 oz.) button mushrooms

1 package (10 oz.) frozen peas, cooked following label directions
1 Tbs. butter
4 eggs
2 canned pimientos, cut in strips

Melt butter in a large, flat, ovenproof dish. Wrap slices of boiled ham around asparagus stalks, which have been divided into 4 portions, and form rolls. Place 2 rolls at either end of dish and top each with a slice of tomato and button mushrooms. Place cooked peas at both ends of dish, next to ham rolls and dot with 1 tablespoon butter. Break eggs into center of dish and garnish with pimiento strips. Bake in a preheated moderate (350°F.) oven until eggs are just set, about 10 to 15 minutes.

Makes 4 servings.

Huevos Potosinos
Eggs San Luis Potosi Style

A very convenient supper dish to have on hand when somebody is going to be late getting home. Try it with a green salad and a favorite dessert.

1 green bell pepper	1 cup light cream
2 Tbs. lard	6 hard-cooked eggs, sliced
½ medium onion, minced	2 cups diced cooked ham
1 cun (10¾ oz.) cream of tomato soup	Salt and pepper to taste
¼ tsp. baking soda	1 tsp. oregano
½ tsp. sugar	6 fried tortillas or slices of buttered toast
1 cup milk, scalded	
1 cup shredded Swiss cheese	

Boil green pepper for 10 minutes. Seed and cut in strips. Melt lard in skillet and add minced onion. When tender but not brown, add pepper strips and stir over moderate heat for 2 or 3 minutes. Transfer mixture to a large saucepan and add soup, baking soda, sugar, milk, shredded cheese, cream, sliced eggs and ham, together with salt, pepper and oregano. Reheat and serve on tortillas or toast. Mixture will keep for an hour or so in top part of double boiler if set over hot, not boiling, water.

Makes 6 servings.

Chili Quiche

1 lb. *chorizos* or sweet Italian sausage links	1½ cups hot milk
4 eggs	2 tsp. chili powder
1½ cups shredded Monterey Jack or Cheddar cheese	1 unbaked 9-inch pie shell with a high fluted rim

Slice sausage into ½-inch thick slices. Place in a large skillet and fry until well browned; drain on paper towels and set aside. In a medium bowl lightly beat eggs. Stir in cheese, milk, chili powder and half of the reserved sausages; set aside. Bake pie shell in a preheated hot oven (400°F.) for 5 minutes. Turn egg mixture into pie shell. Bake for 20 minutes. Place remaining half of sausage slices around outer edge of pie; bake 15 minutes longer or until knife inserted in center comes out clean and top is nicely browned. Let stand 5 minutes before cutting. Serve hot.

Makes 6 servings.

A nice idea for lunch or supper, chili quiche can be made ahead and frozen.

Corn 4

Corn occupies a special place in the Mexican cuisine. Not only is it the staff of life, to nourish and sustain, but because of the skill and ingenuity of Indian cooks, it is the mainstay of dishes that delight the eye as well as the palate.

With the exception of dessert, perhaps, a dish made from *masa* or corn dough is perfectly at home with any course of a meal, from appetizer and soup to main dish and salad. Tortillas, enchiladas, tacos, *quesadillas*—all are for people who like to eat well and also for people who like to cook.

A simple, natural food, corn lends itself to an imaginative range of flavors achieved by adding herbs and condiments. So this is what we have today—an astonishing variety of dishes that are deeply satisfying.

Tortillas

Daily bread, an edible plate to hold other foods, a scoop for gathering up savory beans and sauces—tortillas function as all of them. No wonder they hold the affection of millions.

2 cups *masa harina* (corn flour)   1 tsp. salt
1⅓ cups (approximately) warm water

Blend flour and salt, then add water gradually to form a soft dough. Divide into small balls about 2 inches in diameter. Place a ball of dough between two sheets of waxed paper in a tortilla press and flatten to about 5 to 6 inches in diameter. Place tortilla in ungreased cast-iron skillet or *comal* and cook over moderate heat about 2 minutes on each side, until slightly browned.

Makes 1 dozen tortillas.

Tortillas de los Norteamericanos
Tortillas of the North Americans

If *masa harina* is unavailable, this adaptation, while not authentic, will give a very good version of the "real McCoy." You can make all tortillas hours ahead. Set the oven temperature at warm or 150°F. Wrap tortillas in paper towels as you bake them, then in a cloth napkin that has been wrung out in hot water. When you have a dozen stacked up, dampen the napkin again in hot water and then wrap the entire package in aluminum foil and place in the oven until needed.

Tortillas are the basis for Mexico's most famous dishes.

2 cups flour (all purpose)
1 tsp. salt
1 tsp. baking powder
1½ Tbs. lard

¾ cup (approximately) ice water

Blend together all the dry ingredients. Rub in lard as for pastry making until mixture resembles coarse cornmeal. Slowly trickle ice water down the side of the bowl, blending with a fork. Divide dough into 12 pieces. Remove each piece of dough formed to a sheet of waxed paper until all the dry ingredients are mixed. Shape each into a ball and roll out on lightly floured board as thin as possible. Heat a cast-iron skillet and cook the tortillas one at a time over moderate heat, about 2 minutes on each side. Serve hot and spread with butter.

Makes 1 dozen tortillas.

Enchiladas de Pollo
Chicken Enchiladas

If you're searching for new ways to serve leftover chicken or turkey, here's your answer. It's delicious—and different!

2 cups ground cooked chicken or turkey
½ can (4 oz.) California green chilies, rinsed and finely chopped
1 can (7 oz.) *salsa verde* (green chili sauce)

2 cups heavy cream
½ tsp. salt
4 Tbs. lard
12 tortillas
1½ cups shredded Monterey Jack or Swiss cheese

Combine ground chicken or turkey with rinsed and chopped chilies and green chili sauce. Blend cream with salt. In a skillet, heat lard until moderately hot and dip tortillas in, one at a time, for a few seconds. Then dip in salted cream. Divide chicken mixture onto each tortilla, spread and roll up. Place together in flat, lightly greased baking dish. Pour salted cream over and sprinkle with grated cheese. Bake in preheated moderate (350°F.) oven for 15 to 20 minutes.

Makes 6 servings.

Enchiladas Tampiqueñas
Enchiladas Tampico Style

Just to prove that Mexican cooks aren't creatures of habit, these enchiladas are folded like turnovers instead of rolled up.

12 tortillas
Oil for frying
½ lb. Swiss or Cheddar cheese, cubed
1 cup sour cream
4 cups tomato puree

1 tsp. coriander powder
12 ripe, pitted olives
2 hard-cooked eggs, sliced

Brown tortillas lightly in hot oil and drain on paper towels. Blend together cheese and sour cream. Combine tomato puree and coriander powder and stir into cheese and sour cream, blending well. For those who like a definite salty taste, you may want to add a teaspoon of salt at this point, not forgetting that the cheese contains a certain amount of salt. Place 2 tablespoons of mixture on each tortilla and fold over like a turnover. Arrange in shallow baking dish and bake in moderate oven (350°F.) for 15 to 20 minutes or until cheese is melted. Serve with garnish of olives and slices of egg.

This is very good as a main dish served with a green salad.

Makes 6 servings.

Enfrijoladas
Bean Enchiladas

These enchiladas may be filled with leftover meat, cubed, or cheese or even fried *chorizo* slices. With a tossed green salad and fruit for dessert, you'll have a complete meal.

18 tortillas	3 cups cubed left-over meat, chicker or cheese
Oil for frying	
2 Tbs. lard	
1 medium onion, minced	2 cups refried beans (recipe on page 65)
2 cups solid-pack tomatoes	
2 cups chili relish	1 pint sour cream blended with 1 tsp. salt

Place tortillas, two at a time, in hot oil and fry on both sides until golden brown. Drain on paper towels. Add lard to hot pan and, when heated, add onion and cook until wilted. Add tomatoes and chili relish and cook a few minutes before adding cubed meat or chicken. Spread tortillas with this filling and fold over. Place in heat-proof shallow glass dish with flap side down. Cover with refried beans and then spoon salted sour cream over surface. Bake in a moderate (350°F.) oven for 15 to 20 minutes.

Makes 9 or 10 servings.

Esther Pivnick's Enchiladas Suizas
Swiss Enchiladas

Like many good dishes, this one has traveled a lot—from Switzerland to Mexico and now to the United States, where it is very welcome. Many a hostess has made her reputation with Swiss enchiladas.

2½ cups chopped, cooked chicken	Lard or salad oil for frying
1 can (4 oz.) green chilies	12 tortillas
	2 cups light cream
1 can (7 oz.) green chili sauce	2 cups shredded Swiss cheese

Mix together chicken and chilies, which have

Swiss Enchiladas.

been rinsed in cold water and then minced. Blend with chili sauce. Heat lard or oil in heavy skillet and fry tortillas until golden in color and limp. Fill each with chicken mixture and roll. Place in ungreased baking pan with flap side down. Pour cream over and sprinkle with grated cheese. Bake uncovered in a moderate (350°F.) oven 15 to 20 minutes or until heated through and cheese is melted.

Makes 8 to 12 servings.

Tacos

The most popular of all the *antojitos* ("little whims" or appetizers), tacos are also a good luncheon dish and are at the top of the list for snacking. You'll find them in *taquerías* (similar to our burger stands) and among the staples of every food vendor. Basically, the taco is a warm tortilla folded over a cooked, shredded meat filling and drenched with a sauce of your choice. Then there are the fried tacos. Lightly filled and secured with a toothpick, they are then fried in hot lard. They may be served with *guacamole* or dairy sour cream.

Filling for tacos

1 large tomato *or* ¾ cup canned tomatoes
½ medium onion
3 *serrano* chilies *or* 1 tsp. chili powder
3 sprigs fresh coriander (optional)
1 tsp. salt
2 Tbs. water
2 cups shredded, cooked pork or chicken
Guacamole sauce or sour cream

Chop fresh tomato with onion, chilies and coriander. Blend in salt and water. Add shredded cooked chicken or pork and stir in saucepan over moderate heat until hot. Do not allow to boil.

Enough filling for 6 tacos.

Filling for tacos

It's the custom in Mexico for diners to fill their own tacos at the table if using the soft tortillas. After they are spread with the filling, they can be rolled into a tube and served either with a sauce or topped with shredded lettuce and chopped onion.

3 *chorizos or* hot Italian sausage
3 canned *jalapeño* chilies *or* 2 tsp. chili powder
2 medium potatoes
Tomato sauce from previous recipe

Remove meat from sausage casing. Break up and cook in skillet over low heat until cooked through, about 10 minutes. Do not allow to get hard and overcooked. Remove from pan with slotted spoon. Blend with chilies, which you have chopped, or chili powder and reserve. Peel potatoes and cut in cubes, about ¼-inch on a side. Pat with paper towels to get rid of excess moisture. Reheat rendered fat from sausages and add potatoes. Let cook until golden brown and tender, turning occasionally. Blend with sausage mixture and tomato sauce from previous recipe.

Enough filling for 8 to 10 tacos.

Tacos de Res
Beef Tacos

While beef is not the most commonly used meat in Mexico, it appears once in a while in a particularly savory dish. A gentle reminder for these days when we are all watching the food budget—fillings for tacos offer an interesting and economical way of using up leftover meats. They combine very well with hamburger, too!

1 cup chopped onion
2 Tbs. salad oil
2 Tbs. flour
2 chopped *poblano* chilies *or* 3 Tbs. chili powder
1 cup canned tomatoes
2 cups ground cooked beef *or* 1 lb. hamburger, cooked
1 cup light cream
1 tsp. salt
12 tacos

Sauté half the onion in hot oil until soft, not brown. Remove pan from heat while you stir in flour and chilies or chili powder. Return to heat and stir 5 minutes. Add canned tomatoes and cooked, ground beef. Cover and simmer until thick, about 5 minutes. Add cream and remaining raw onion and salt. Heat but do not allow to boil, as cream may curdle. Fill into tacos and top with grated cheese or shredded lettuce and a little chopped onion.

Yield: 12 tacos.

Elegant Chili Tacos

1 Tbs. instant minced onion
¼ tsp. instant minced garlic
6 Tbs. water
2 Tbs. olive or salad oil
1½ lbs. boneless round steak, cut into ½-inch cubes
1½ Tbs. flour
1 can (1 lb.) tomatoes, broken up
1 cup diced, peeled and cored apple
2 Tbs. raisins
1½ tsp. chili powder
¾ tsp. salt
1/16 tsp. ground cinnamon
1/16 tsp. ground cloves
12 prepared taco shells

Rehydrate minced onion and garlic in 3 tablespoons water for 10 minutes. In a large skillet heat oil. Add meat; sauté until nicely browned. Add onion and garlic; sauté 3 minutes. Stir in flour. Add tomatoes, apple, raisins, chili powder, salt, cinnamon, cloves and remaining 3 tablespoons water. Cover and cook, stirring occasionally, for 10 minutes. Spoon mixture into taco shells. Garnish with shredded lettuce and shredded Monterey Jack cheese, if desired.

Makes 6 servings.

Tacos Verdes, Blancos, y Colorados
Green, White and Red Tacos

When you are in the mood for a real Mexican fiesta, there's nothing like a main dish with the colors of the Mexican flag.

12 tortillas
Oil for frying
2½ cups cooked turkey, diced
3 Tbs. grated Swiss cheese
1 cup sour cream
1 tsp. salt
Tomato sauce (recipe below)
1½ cups *guacamole* (recipe on page 21)

Fry tortillas lightly in oil until heated through but not crisp. Drain on paper towels. Blend together cubed turkey and grated cheese and divide mixture onto tortillas. Roll up each and arrange on hot platter, flap side down. Over top spread a layer of sour cream that has been blended with salt, a layer of tomato sauce and a layer of *guacamole,* each arranged in strips of equal width. Heat in moderate oven (350°F.) for about 15 minutes or until hot enough to serve.

Makes about 8 servings.

Tomato sauce

2 Tbs. oil
1 medium onion, chopped
2 cups tomato puree
2 Tbs. chili sauce
2 tsp. salt

Heat oil in heavy skillet. Add onion and cook over moderate heat until wilted. Add remaining ingredients and cook, stirring occasionally, until sauce is thick.

Tacos de Carne Molida
Ground Beef Tacos

You might prefer to eat these "out of hand" with a little taco sauce dribbled over all. This may sound more American than Mexican, but so what?

The way to stuff a taco and (below) the finished product.

2 Tbs. lard	1 clove garlic,
1 large onion,	pressed
chopped	2 Tbs. chili relish
1 lb. ground beef	1 tsp. oregano
1 green pepper,	1 tsp. vinegar
chopped	2-3 tsp. salt
1 cup solid-pack	12 tortillas
tomatoes	Oil for frying tortillas

Heat lard and add chopped onion and ground beef. Cook over moderate heat, stirring constantly. Add green pepper, tomatoes, pressed garlic, chili relish, oregano, vinegar and salt and continue to cook over moderate heat, stirring occasionally, for 15 minutes. Warm tortillas in a slow oven (250°F.) to soften. Divide meat mixture onto the tortillas and spread to cover almost to the edge of each. Roll and place seam side down in hot oil, frying to desired crispness. May be served with avocado wedges, if desired, and shredded lettuce.

Makes 6 to 12 servings.

Tostados

Tostados are good for snacking or as a luncheon dish. When made in miniature, they also make very attractive appetizers, or *antojitos*.

6 tortillas, about 5	1 cup cooked,
inches in diame-	shredded chicken
ter	1 cup shredded
3 Tbs. lard, heated	lettuce
1 cup refried beans	6 slices tomato
(page 65)	½ cup grated cheese
1 *jalapeño* chili,	Radishes
canned, chopped,	½ cup sour cream
or ½ green bell	(optional)
pepper, chopped	

Fry tortillas on both sides in hot lard until lightly browned. Spread with a layer of refried beans and sprinkle with chopped chili or chopped green bell pepper. Cover with a layer of shredded, cooked chicken and garnish with shredded lettuce, tomato slices, grated cheese and radishes. Serve with sour cream if desired.

Makes 6 tostados.

More Fillings for Tostados

¼ cup salad oil (not	1 cup cooked, canned
olive oil)	crabmeat, shredded
½ medium onion,	3 Tbs. finely chopped
finely chopped	fresh coriander, if
½ cup celery, finely	available
chopped	1 tsp. salt
5 canned *serrano*	
chilies *or* 1 green	
bell pepper with 1	
tsp. chili powder	

Heat oil in skillet and add chopped onion. Stir over moderate heat until onion is tender but not brown. Add chopped celery and chilies or bell pepper with chili powder and stir until all ingredients are a very light brown. Then blend in fresh coriander, crabmeat, and salt.

Enough to cover 6 tostados.

3 Tbs. lard	2 hard-cooked eggs,
1 medium onion, chop-	sliced
ped	1 tsp. salt
1 clove garlic,	¼ tsp. pepper, freshly
minced	ground
1 cup canned red	
kidney beans	

Heat lard over moderate heat in skillet. Add onion and garlic and stir until onion is tender, not brown. Add red kidney beans, sliced eggs, salt and pepper and heat through. When hot, spread over tostados.

Enough for 6 to 8 tostados.

Tostados de Frijol y Chorizo
Tostados with Refried Beans and Chorizo

The Mexicans seem to be very fond of serving a hot dish with a cold garnish, and this tastes much better than it sounds. There's nothing mysterious about *chorizo*—it's the Spanish sausage that is very well seasoned. If this isn't available near you, try the Italian hot sausage instead.

1 lb. *chorizo*	2 cups tomato sauce
1 medium onion, chopped	3 Tbs. Parmesan cheese, grated
12 tostados	Shredded lettuce
2 cups refried beans (recipe page 65)	Avocado wedges
	Radishes

Remove casing from *chorizo* and cut meat in ¼-inch slices. Fry without added fat. When meat starts to brown, add chopped onion and cook until onion is translucent and wilted.

Blend in tomato sauce. Spread tostados with hot beans. Then spread the onion and sausage mixture over the beans and cover with grated cheese. Top with lettuce and garnish with avocado wedges and radishes.

Makes 6 or 12 servings, depending on how hungry your guests are.

Tostados de Vigilia
Tostados for Lent

As the name implies, tostados are tortillas that have been fried. You can get them canned or in boxes in Mexican stores, already prepared, or make them at home by frying tortillas and then folding over to leave plenty of space for filling. While these were meant for Lenten serving originally, no law says you can't serve them any time.

1 can (7 oz.) tuna	6 tostados
1 Tbs. minced onion	1 cup sliced, cooked summer squash or zucchini
2 canned California green chilies, chopped	1½ cups chili sauce
2 Tbs. vinegar	Shredded lettuce

Break up contents of can of tuna with a fork. Add onion, chopped chilies and vinegar and mix well. Fill tostados with this mixture and top with cooked squash slices. Serve with chili sauce and shredded lettuce.

Makes 6 servings.

Quesadillas

Quesadillas are small turnovers of tortilla dough, stuffed with a variety of fillings. They are cooked either on a *comal*, a flat, cast-iron skillet or fried in lard. If you prefer to avoid fried foods, you can substitute a skillet or griddle for the *comal*.

Quesadilla dough

1½ cups *masa harina* (see page 35)
1 cup minus 2 Tbs. water

Add water slowly to the *masa harina* to form a fairly soft dough. Divide dough into 12 portions and shape each into a ball the size of a walnut. Place a plastic bag on the inside of each plate of your tortilla press and press each ball of dough out to a rather thick tortilla, about 4½ inches in diameter. Remove top plastic bag and place 1 tablespoon filling on *quesadilla* away from the edges. Lift up bottom bag and use it to flip over and fold the dough in half to form a half-moon shape. Take the *quesadilla* in your hands and gently press the edges to seal. Cook on *comal* or skillet over moderate heat, turning to brown both sides, or fry in hot lard. If made ahead, store in a damp cloth to prevent drying out.

Makes enough for 12 *quesadillas*.

Fillings for Twelve Quesadillas

2 Tbs. lard	2 tsp. chili powder
2 medium potatoes, peeled and diced	1 tsp. salt
½ green bell pepper, chopped	Freshly ground black pepper
½ lb. ground beef	¼ tsp. Tabasco sauce

Melt lard in large skillet. When hot, add peeled and diced potatoes and cook over moderate heat until golden brown, stirring every 2 or 3 minutes. Add chopped green pepper and stir another 2 minutes. Blend ground beef with remaining ingredients and stir into potato mixture. Cook, still stirring, just until meat loses its red color.

2 Tbs. lard	1 Tbs. chili powder
1 canned pimiento, chopped	Salt and pepper to taste
2 large tomatoes, peeled and chopped	12 slices Muenster cheese
2 cloves garlic, minced	2 ripe avocados, sliced
6 scallions with green part, chopped	1 small onion, chopped

Heat lard in large skillet. Add pimiento, tomatoes, garlic, scallions, chili powder, salt and pepper. Stir over moderate heat until mixture thickens. Add cheese slices and mix well. Heat *quesadillas* and add filling, following directions on page 41. Fry on both sides in additional hot lard and garnish with avocado slices and chopped onion.

Tamales

Tamales have a long history, going back to the very early inhabitants of Mexico. They are fiesta food, the ceremonial food on November 2, the Day of the Dead, and the "Sunday Night Special" in many restaurants. The traditional tamale is steamed in corn husks. These can be purchased dried (see Sources of Supply, page 93). If you choose the fresh husk, be sure to trim off the cupped part at the base and cut off the pointed tip. The dried husks will reach you looking very papery, so pour plenty of hot water over them and let stand several hours to soften. Before using, shake well and pat dry with a clean dish towel. You can also use a special paper (*papel de tamales*), available by mail, but regular parchment paper used for cooking will do nicely.

You will need, for best results, an electric blender, an electric mixer and a steamer.

Since it is difficult to find the large, white corn kernels favored by Mexican cooks, a satisfactory substitute is the Quaker brand of quick grits. They give a flavor that is not exactly authentic but the texture is very good.

Preparing the husk for tamales.

Basic tamale dough

1 lb. Quaker Quick Grits	1½ to 1¾ cups strong chicken broth, lukewarm
2 tsp. salt	
½ lb. lard	½ tsp. baking powder

Grind grits as fine as possible in the blender. Add salt and mix well. Beat lard in electric mixer 5 minutes. Gradually add grits to beaten lard, alternately with chicken broth. If broth is too warm, it may melt the lard. If this happens, place mixture in refrigerator a few minutes to firm up. Add baking powder and blend well.

Makes enough dough for about 3 dozen tamales, 3 inches long.

Making tamales

Tear some of the prepared husks lengthwise into narrow strips for tying. Spread a thin coating of tamale dough over the broadest part of the prepared husks, to within 1½ inches of base and within about 3 inches of tip. Spread filling down center of husk and fold sides firmly together. Turn up the pointed end of husk and fold the broader end over it, just like wrapping a package. Tie each tamale firmly across the flap with the strips of husk. Each package should be watertight. Stack tamales upright in the top part of the steamer, with tied flaps upward. Pack firmly but not too tightly as the filling swells in cooking. Cover tamales with more corn husks, then top with waxed paper or some old toweling to absorb condensed moisture from the lid. Place top of steamer over the base, which is ¾ filled with boiling water. Cover with tight-fitting lid and cook 2½ to 3 hours. The water should keep a gentle bubble, not a full, rolling boil. Refill with boiling water from time to time. One way to tell if your heat is too low is to put a coin in the water. When the water is bubbling, you'll hear it rattle.

To test tamales for doneness, remove one from the center and another from the side of the pan. In each, the dough should separate easily from the husk and have a smooth and spongy texture. So you wanted to "cook Mexican." This is a real production!

Serving tamales

They are very good eaten "as is" when freshly cooked and can take the place of potatoes or other starchy food in the menu. When cool, they can be heated gently while still in their husks, in an ungreased skillet. Just keep turning them so that they heat evenly. Tamales can be refrigerated for about a week while still in their husks, but if they are to be kept for a longer period of time, better wrap them in foil and freeze. To reheat, put foil package, still frozen, in a moderate (350°F.) oven for about 30 minutes.

Savory Suggestions for Filling Tamales

¾ cup salad oil (not   Few grains cayenne
   olive oil)   pepper

¾ cup flour   1¼ cups hot chili
2 cloves garlic,   sauce (canned)
   crushed   1 tsp. salt
1½ cups canned   2 tsp. oregano
   tomato sauce   3 cups ground,
2 medium onions,   cooked meat
   peeled and   2 tsp. chili powder
   chopped

Heat oil in large skillet and stir in flour. When flour is a golden brown (do not allow to get dark), add crushed garlic, tomato sauce, chopped onions, hot chili sauce, salt, oregano, meat, chili powder and cayenne pepper. Cook over low heat, uncovered, for 30 minutes or until sauce is quite thick. It should be stirred occasionally while cooking.

Makes approximately 6 cups of sauce.

2 cups cooked,   2 Tbs. capers
   minced chicken or ½ cup canned tomato
   turkey   sauce
¼ cup chopped
   almonds

Tamales, with husks and filling in background.

1 cup canned red
kidney beans
½ cup finely diced,
cooked ham
½ cup canned tomato
sauce

¼ cup finely diced
Muenster cheese
½ tsp. Tabasco sauce

5 or 6 strips crisply
cooked bacon
1 tsp. chili powder
½ cup finely diced
Muenster cheese

½ cup canned tomato
sauce

Crumble bacon. In fat rendered from bacon, place chili powder and stir over low heat for 1 minute. Blend with bacon and remaining ingredients.

Cazuela de Tamales
Tamale Casserole

A make-ahead casserole is always welcome. This *cazuela* fits very well into a buffet menu or a Sunday night supper. There's another "plus" in its favor—it's an excellent way to use up leftover chicken, turkey or meat.

1 dozen large
tamales
2 cups diced, cooked
meat or poultry
1 can (1 lb.) kernel
corn, drained

½ lb. Muenster
cheese, sliced
¼ cup heavy cream
1 can (15 oz.) tomato
sauce
Corn chips

Slice tamales in half lengthwise. Lightly oil a 3- to 4-quart casserole and place a layer of tamale slices in it. Cover with a layer of diced, cooked meat or poultry. You may wish to add a little salt and pepper to the meat if it is not already seasoned. Cover with a layer of kernel corn and then cheese. Repeat until ingredients are used, then pour cream and tomato sauce over all. Top with a layer of corn chips. Place in a moderate (350°F.) oven until heated through, about 30 minutes.

Makes 8 to 10 servings.

Tamale Pie

2 Tbs. instant
minced onion

1 can (1 lb., 1 oz.)
whole kernel corn,
drained

¼ tsp. instant minced
garlic
2 Tbs. water
2 Tbs. olive oil
1 lb. ground lean
beef
1 can (1 lb., 12 oz.)
tomatoes, broken
up
¾ cup cornmeal

¾ cup pitted ripe
olives, chopped
4 tsp. chili powder
1 tsp. salt
¼ tsp. ground black
pepper
1 cup shredded
Monterey Jack or
Cheddar cheese

Rehydrate onion and garlic in water for 10 minutes. In a large skillet heat oil. Add onion and garlic and sauté 3 minutes. Add beef and sauté 5 minutes or until beef is browned; set aside. In a saucepan heat tomatoes; stir in cornmeal. Cook, stirring constantly, until thickened, about 10 minutes. Blend in corn, olives, chili powder, salt, black pepper and reserved cooked meat mixture. Turn into a greased 2-quart casserole. Top with cheese. Bake in a preheated moderate oven (350°F.) 40 minutes or until cheese is bubbly and golden. Let rest 10 minutes before serving. If desired, garnish with whole olives.

Makes 4 to 6 servings.

Tamales de Dulce
Sweet Tamales

These are very good for a substantial breakfast dish or as a snack with a cup of hot chocolate. Please don't try to serve them as dessert; coming after a full meal, the flavor would not be appreciated.

Use half the recipe for basic tamale dough (page 42), substituting ½ pound butter for ½ pound lard. Even though these tamales are sweet, you still use the chicken broth in the dough. After the dough has been moistened, blend in the following ingredients.

1 Tbs. cinnamon
½ cup sugar

¾ cup chopped
walnuts
¾ cup raisins

Mix all ingredients and blend into tamale dough. Follow directions on page 43 for spreading on the husks and steaming them.

Makes about 2 dozen sweet tamales.

Pan de Cebolla y Maíz
Onion Corn Bread

If you love corn sticks, the following batter will make about 2 dozen. Spoon them into hot, greased, corn-stick pans. Otherwise bake this corn bread in a well-greased 8×8×2-inch baking dish.

1½ cups cornmeal
½ cup flour
¼ cup finely minced onion
1 tsp. baking powder
2 tsp. sugar
2 eggs, beaten
1 tsp. salt
1 tsp. soda
2 cups buttermilk
3 Tbs. melted shortening

Combine dry ingredients in a mixing bowl. Blend beaten eggs, buttermilk and melted shortening. Mix thoroughly with dry ingredients. Pour into well-greased 8×8×2-inch baking dish. Bake in preheated hot oven (425°F.) 15 to 20 minutes or until browned. Serve hot.

Makes 6 to 8 servings.

Fish 5

Pescado en Salsa de Naranja
Fish with Orange Sauce

The French have their specialty of fillet of sole with fruit—little seedless grapes. The Mexicans are just as inventive with a fruit sauce that goes well with whatever white fish you may have on hand—sole, flounder, cod or halibut. Just remember not to overcook, and keep in mind that thin fillets take much less time than hefty fish steaks.

6 fillets of sole or flounder or fish steaks	2 large tomatoes
1 lemon	1 medium onion, minced
Salt and white pepper to taste	4 large oranges
¼ cup olive oil	2 dozen stuffed olives
	6 gherkins

Wash fish and refrigerate for 1 hour with juice of 1 lemon poured over. Sprinkle with salt and white pepper (black pepper will give you black speckles you don't want in this dish). Pour 2 tablespoons oil in baking dish and place fish on it. Chop tomatoes and cover fish with them, then add minced onion and remaining olive oil. Bake in a preheated moderate oven (350°F.). Allow 12 to 15 minutes for fillet of sole or flounder, longer for fish steaks, depending on their thickness, but for goodness' sake, don't overcook. Squeeze and strain juice of 2 oranges over fish before serving. Garnish with remaining oranges cut in sections along with olives and gherkins.

Makes 6 servings.

Pescado a la Veracruzana
Fish with Hot Sauce, Veracruz Style

If you think 2 tablespoons of chili powder will be overwhelming, cut the amount in half; the sauce will still be lively. This dish has a definite flavor of Spain and at one time was considered one of the better-known triumphs of Spanish kitchen economy. Alas, nothing is inexpensive anymore!

½ cup olive oil	2 Tbs. chili powder
½ small onion, minced	½ tsp. sugar

2 cloves garlic,
minced
2 cups tomato sauce
Pinch of cayenne
pepper
⅛ tsp. cinnamon
¼ tsp. ground cloves

3 medium potatoes,
boiled and cubed
6 fish fillets or slices
¼ cup olive oil
3 slices white bread
1 lemon, cut in
wedges

Heat ¼ cup olive oil in skillet and cook onion and garlic until tender but not brown. Transfer to a large saucepan and add tomato sauce, cayenne pepper, cinnamon, cloves, chili powder, sugar and cubed potatoes. Stir gently over moderate heat. If sauce seems very thick, add 2 or 3 tablespoons water. Heat another ¼ cup olive oil in skillet and brown fish on both sides. When cooked, place on serving platter and pour sauce over. Keep hot. Cut each slice of bread into 2 triangles. Heat remaining ¼ cup olive oil and fry bread until golden on both sides. Use to garnish fish and serve with lemon wedges.

Makes 6 servings.

Pescado en Salsa
Fish in Sauce

This is a variation on a theme—that is, if you enjoy using the convenient "instants" such as dehydrated onion and garlic. There are times when the clock rushes you to get a good main dish ready in a hurry, and here is a solution!

2 Tbs. instant
minced onion
¼ tsp. instant
minced garlic
2 Tbs. water
1 chicken bouillon
cube
1 cup boiling water

1½ lbs. fish fillets,
fresh, or frozen
and thawed
2 Tbs. salad oil
1 cup soft bread
crumbs
1 tsp. chili powder
½ tsp. paprika
¼ tsp. ground cumin

Rehydrate onion and garlic in water for 10 minutes; set aside. In a large skillet, dissolve bouillon cube in boiling water. Add fish fillets. Cover and simmer (do not let boil) for 10 minutes or until fish flakes easily when tested with a fork. Remove fish to a hot platter and keep warm. Heat oil in skillet and add reserved onion and garlic. Sauté for 3 minutes over moderate heat, stirring. Add broth from fish (about 1 cup), bread crumbs, chili powder, paprika and cumin. Stir well. Bring to boiling

point. Reduce heat and simmer, uncovered, for 2 minutes, stirring occasionally. Pour over fish. May be garnished with parsley if desired.

Makes 4 servings.

Pescado en Salsa de Almendras
Fish in Almond Sauce

A typical touch of Mexico is the use of nuts for thickening a sauce. You can substitute walnuts for the almonds in this recipe if you prefer. A Mouli grater comes in handy here, for if you try to grate nuts in the blender, you might very well end up with an oily paste.

6 fish fillets, fresh or
frozen
Salt and pepper to
taste
Juice of 1 lemon
¼ cup melted butter
¼ cup ground al-
monds or walnuts

¼ cup milk
¼ cup cream
1 cup grated, mild
Cheddar cheese
⅛ tsp. cinnamon
¼ cup dry bread
crumbs

Place fish in lightly greased baking dish. Sprinkle with salt and pepper and pour lemon juice over. Refrigerate 20 minutes. Brush fish with melted butter. Blend together ground nuts, milk, cream and grated cheese and spread over fish. Blend cinnamon and bread crumbs and sprinkle over fish. Bake in moderately hot oven (375°F.) about 30 minutes or until fish flakes easily when tested with a fork.

Makes 6 servings.

Frituras de Camarones con Salsa Picante
Shrimp Fritters with Savory Sauce

A different and very savory way of expanding a small amount of shrimp into a family-sized dish. You might also want to file this under your list of appetizers, since the fritters, made on a miniature scale, are very good for nibbling.

2 cups canned or
cooked shrimp
8 eggs, separated
1 small onion
1 clove garlic
1 tsp. salt
1 tsp. chili powder

2 Tbs. chopped
parsley
½ green pepper,
finely chopped
5 Tbs. flour
Lard for deep frying
Paprika

Cut up shrimp and place in blender with egg yolks, a small amount at a time. Blend until mixture is smooth and then stir in onion, garlic, salt, chili powder, parsley, chopped green pepper and flour. Beat egg whites until stiff but not dry and carefully fold into shrimp mixture. Drop by tablespoons into hot fat (at least 375°F.) and fry until golden on both sides. Drain on paper towels and sprinkle with paprika. Serve with hot chili sauce.

Makes 6 servings.

Chili sauce for shrimp fritters

6 Tbs. butter	2 cups canned,
2 medium onions,	sieved, solid-
chopped	pack tomatoes
2 green peppers,	2 Tbs. chili powder
finely chopped	2 cups beef broth
2 cloves garlic,	Salt and pepper to
minced	taste
¼ cup flour	2 tsp. dried basil

Melt butter in skillet and fry onions, green peppers and garlic until tender but not brown. Mix flour with a little sieved tomato and the chili powder to form a smooth paste. Combine with remaining tomatoes, beef broth, salt, pepper and basil. Simmer, covered, for about 10 minutes.

Makes approximately 4 cups of sauce.

Camarones en Salsa Mexicana
Shrimp in Mexican Sauce

This is a special dish you'll enjoy serving to guests, especially since all the preparation is done ahead. Good accompaniments are plain boiled rice topped with some of the shrimp marinade and a green vegetable.

2 lbs. raw shrimp	3 cloves garlic,
1 cup salad oil	minced
2 tsp. chili powder	1 tsp. salt
mixed with 1 Tbs.	4 tsp. basil
vinegar	1 Tbs. chopped fresh
¼ tsp. freshly ground	mint leaves *or* 1 tsp.
pepper	dried mint

Wash, shell and devein shrimp. Make a marinade of oil, chili powder that has been mixed to a paste with vinegar, pepper, garlic, salt, basil and chopped mint. Pour marinade over shrimp and refrigerate, covered, overnight or at least 6 hours. Place shrimp with marinade in a heat-proof shallow dish and place under broiler, about 5 inches from source of heat. Broil 6 to 10 minutes, depending on size, turning once while they cook. Serve with as much marinade as you prefer.

Makes 6 servings.

Ensalada de Camarones
Shrimp Salad

This is a refreshing and colorful salad to serve when the temperature is zooming. You prepare the shrimp mixture hours ahead, then garnish with sliced avocado, tomato wedges and lemon slices at the last minute.

¾ cup salad oil	2 lbs. raw shrimp,
½ cup finely chopped	peeled and de-
onion	veined
1 clove garlic,	Lettuce
minced	1 avocado, sliced
⅓ cup white vinegar	2 large tomatoes, cut
1 Tbs. chili powder	in wedges
1 tsp. sugar	1 lemon, thinly
1 tsp. salt	sliced
Pinch cayenne	
pepper	

In a large skillet, heat 2 tablespoons of the oil and sauté onion and garlic until tender but not brown. Place in a bowl and add another ½ cup oil, vinegar, chili powder, sugar, salt and cayenne pepper and mix well. Heat remaining 2 tablespoons oil in skillet, add shrimp and sauté until pink. Add to bowl with marinade and mix carefully so that each shrimp is covered. Cover bowl and refrigerate at least 4 hours. Drain and place in salad bowl lined with lettuce. Garnish with avocado slices, tomato wedges and thin slices of lemon.

Makes 6 servings.

Ensalada Mexicana
Mexican Salad

Acapulco is famous for the sport of tuna fishing, and hotels are adorned with photographs of guests with their prize catches. We settle for the canned variety. Probably not as much fun as catching your own tuna, but it's a lot simpler.

1½ cups canned chunk tuna
2 cups cooked or canned pink beans
½ cup mayonnaise
Salt and pepper to taste
Whole lettuce leaves
4 cups shredded lettuce
3 large tomatoes, peeled and cut in wedges
4 hard-cooked eggs, sliced
6 Tbs. mayonnaise

Separate tuna chunks and mix lightly with beans and ½ cup mayonnaise. Blend in salt and pepper to taste. Line a salad bowl with lettuce leaves, add shredded lettuce and place tuna mixture over this. Garnish with tomato wedges, sliced hard-cooked eggs and mayonnaise.

Makes 4 to 6 servings.

6
Poultry

Poultry in Mexico, as elsewhere, is a staple item in the cook's repertoire, popular both for its versatility and economy. Although it appears in many delicious and original recipes, one dish stands out above all others.

Without a doubt, Turkey in Mole Sauce is the most famous of all classical Mexican dishes. While there are many *mole* sauces, they all have one ingredient in common—chilies and more chilies. There is a legend surrounding this ancient dish; it certainly adds to the interest, but we should take it with a grain of salt. As the story goes, the nuns of the Santa Rosa convent in Puebla created this dish back in the sixteenth century to honor a visiting viceroy and archbishop.

Since in those days, the viceroy was equated with the Spanish king and the archbishop with a high priest, it seems probable that the Indian nuns resurrected a royal Aztec recipe. This famous sauce contains bitter chocolate, and in the days of the Aztecs, chocolate was forbidden to women. Even among the men it was reserved only for royalty, the military nobility and the higher ranks of the priests.

The good nuns must be credited with saving the dish from oblivion, however, and for adding their own refinements such as the Spanish-inspired cinnamon and cloves. While the recipe may have been streamlined over the years, it's still no 1-2-3 concoction, but it's a new taste treat to delight guests and so different from the usual stuffed turkey.

Mole Poblano de Guajolote
Turkey in Mole Sauce

5 *ancho* chilies*
3 *pasilla* chilies*
4 *mulato* chilies*
1 small turkey, about 8 lbs., cut in serving-size pieces
5 Tbs. lard
2 large onions, chopped
5 cloves garlic, chopped
1 cup blanched almonds
¾ cup raisins
½ tsp. powdered cloves
½ tsp. ground coriander
½ tsp. anise extract
½ tsp. cinnamon
5 Tbs. sesame seeds
2 sprigs fresh coriander (optional)
1 tortilla or slice of toast, broken up
3 medium tomatoes, peeled, seeded and chopped
2 squares bitter chocolate
Salt and pepper to taste

Ancho, pasilla and *mulato* chilies are all dried, ranging from dark red to brown in color, and all are very pungent. If you can't obtain all three, try to settle for *ancho* together with ¼ teaspoon cayenne pepper. Crumble chilies with fingers and then wash hands immediately to avoid a skin burn.

Cover turkey pieces with salted water, bring to a boil, then reduce heat to simmer and cook 1 hour. Drain and reserve 2 cups turkey stock. Dry turkey pieces well with paper towels. Heat lard in a large skillet and brown turkey, a few pieces at a time. Don't overcrowd the pan. Transfer to a large heat-proof casserole and reserve lard.

Combine onions, garlic, almonds, raisins, powdered cloves, ground coriander, anise extract, cinnamon, *2 tablespoons* of the sesame seeds, fresh coriander, if used, prepared chilies, tortilla or toast and tomatoes. Blend a small amount at a time in blender to make a coarse puree. Reheat fat in skillet, adding more lard if necessary to make about 3 tablespoons. Add puree and stir constantly over moderate heat for 5 minutes. Add the 2 cups of turkey broth, chocolate, salt and pepper to taste, and stir until chocolate has melted. Sauce should be somewhat thicker than heavy cream. Pour sauce over turkey in casserole, cover and cook over very low heat for about 30 minutes or until turkey is tender. Sprinkle with remaining sesame seeds just before serving. Serve with hot tortillas, *guacamole*, refried beans and rice for a truly festive occasion.

Makes 10 to 12 servings.

Party Mole Sauce

Just so that you don't get discouraged over the previous *mole* recipe, here is another version! It's not so authentic, but all the ingredients are readily available.

⅔ cup blanched almonds	½ tsp. instant minced garlic
3 Tbs. sesame seeds	½ tsp. ground cinnamon
1 can (1 lb., 1 oz.) Italian plum tomatoes	¼ tsp. aniseed
	⅛ tsp. ground cloves

½ cup seedless raisins	⅛ tsp. black pepper
½ cup dried onion flakes	3 cups chicken broth, divided
1 slice white toast *or* 1 tortilla, broken up	2 Tbs. lard
3 Tbs. chili powder	1 oz. unsweetened chocolate
1 tsp. salt	2 lbs. sliced, cooked turkey *or* 2 cooked chickens (2½ to 3 lb. each)

In blender jar combine almonds and sesame seeds. Blend until finely ground. Add tomatoes, raisins, onion flakes, toast or tortilla, chili powder, salt, garlic, cinnamon, aniseed, cloves and black pepper. Stir in 1 cup of broth. Blend at high speed until mixture is smooth. In a large skillet heat lard. Pour in tomato mixture and simmer, stirring constantly, for 5 minutes. Add remaining 2 cups chicken broth and chocolate. Reduce heat and cook, uncovered, until chocolate has melted. Add cooked turkey or chicken and simmer, covered, 30 minutes.

Serve sprinkled with additional sesame seeds if desired.

Makes 1½ quarts of sauce.

Guajolote Borracho con Arroz
Drunken Turkey with Rice

Many Mexican dishes carry names that reveal a delightful sense of humor! Browsing through a Mexican cookbook, you might find *Angaripolas*—"A Gaudy Dish" of pigs' feet and nineteen other ingredients. The "Tablecloth Stainer" is chicken or pork in a rich, dark-red sauce, while "Chicken in the Garden" boasts twenty-nine ingredients including seven fruits and seven spices, making the "Garden." "Two Cultures Chicken" suggests past history, while "Drunken Chicken" is baked in wine. Here is a version of "Drunken Turkey."

Minced turkey giblets	2 Tbs. vinegar
4 Tbs. lard	½ cup dry sherry
2 medium onions, cut in rings	½ tsp. chili powder
⅓ cup chopped parsley	1 jar green olives (about 30)
2 Tbs. sesame seeds	2 canned green chilies, rinsed
4 whole black peppercorns	1 to 2 cups turkey stock (from cooked giblets; use larger amount if you prefer a mild sauce)
1-inch stick cinnamon, broken up	
¼ tsp. ground cloves	Paprika
1 bay leaf	1 Tbs. gravy coloring (such as Kitchen Bouquet)
1 tsp. salt	
1 clove garlic, minced	Cooked rice
1 small turkey (about 7 to 8 lbs.), cut in half	

To make stock, simmer giblets in 2½ cups water in covered pan for 1 to 2 hours and set aside.

Heat lard in bottom of dutch oven. Put in onions, parsley, sesame seeds, black peppercorns, cinnamon stick, cloves, bay leaf, salt and minced garlic. Arrange turkey halves in pan, cut side down. Pour vinegar, sherry and half the turkey stock over turkey. Sprinkle chili powder over turkey. Slice half the olives. Cut chilies into thin strips and place them with olives over the turkey. Cover tightly and simmer 1 to 1½ hours (or until tender), turning turkey about every 15 minutes. Remove turkey to platter and keep warm. Sprinkle with paprika. Place contents of pan in jar of blender and puree. Add remaining stock to taste and blend with gravy coloring. Pour over turkey and serve with plain boiled rice.

Makes approximately 8 servings.

Arroz con Pollo
Chicken with Rice

Since chickens are more economical to raise than beef cattle, the Mexican kitchen has evolved a large variety of poultry dishes. *Arroz con Pollo* is a famous classic.

3½-lb. frying chicken, cut in serving-size pieces	2 cloves garlic, minced
Salt and white pepper	2 cups canned tomatoes
4 Tbs. lard	3 canned *serrano* chilies, chopped
1 cup rice	1 tsp. cumin powder
2 medium onions, thinly sliced	¼ tsp. saffron
	4 cups chicken broth
	2 canned pimientos, cut in strips

Rub chicken pieces with salt and white pepper. Heat lard in skillet and brown chicken. Remove to a heat-proof covered casserole. Sauté onions and garlic in skillet, adding more lard if necessary. Cook until onions are limp but not brown. Add to the casserole together with tomatoes, chilies, cumin powder, saffron and chicken broth. Cover casserole and simmer gently on top of stove for 30 minutes.

Add more lard to skillet if necessary and, when hot, add rice. Stir with a wooden spoon for about 2 minutes over moderate heat, then add to the casserole. Cover and continue cooking another 30 minutes or until chicken is tender and all the liquid has been absorbed. Garnish with pimiento strips.

Makes 6 servings.

Tip: When frying chicken, cook just 2 or 3

pieces at a time. Never overcrowd the pan, for this just delays browning. After the rice has been added, reduce heat to simmer. If heat is too high, the liquid will be absorbed too quickly and you are apt to end up with rice not sufficiently cooked.

Pipián Rojo de Ajonjolí
Chicken Fricassee with Sesame Seeds

Pipián is the name given by Mexicans to a sauce that contains ground nuts or seeds and spices. The nuts or seeds help thicken the sauce as well as give it a special flavor. This is a colorful and different approach from the usual pale fricassee.

1 chicken (3 lb.) cut into serving-size pieces	1 Tbs. chili powder
	1 Tbs. paprika
	1 Tbs. onion powder
2½ cups water	½ tsp. garlic powder
1½ tsp. salt	¼ tsp. sugar
½ cup sesame seeds	1 pinch ground cloves
1 Tbs. salad oil	
1 can (8 oz.) tomato sauce	¼ tsp. cinnamon

In a large saucepan combine chicken, water and salt. Cover and simmer until tender, about 30 minutes. Remove chicken from broth; keep meat warm. Reserve 1 cup broth and set aside. In jar of electric blender grind sesame seeds or crush in a mortar and pestle. Heat oil in a large skillet and add sesame seeds. Cook and stir over moderate heat until golden, about 5 minutes. Stir in tomato sauce, chili powder, paprika, onion powder, garlic powder, sugar, cloves and cinnamon. Cook 5 minutes. Stir in reserved broth. Spoon over chicken. Sprinkle with additional sesame seeds if desired.

Makes 4 servings.

Cocido de Pollo de María
María's Chicken Stew

An old hen is more economical to buy than two young chickens, but if you can't spend the time to cook the senior bird, two broiler-fryers will do nicely. If you are using the hen, we suggest you simmer it first for an hour before starting these general directions.

Arroz con Pollo, *another classic in Mexican cooking.*

María's Chicken Stew.

¼ cup flour
1 tsp. salt
Black pepper
2 broiler-fryer chickens (2½ to 3 lb. each), cut in serving-size pieces
¼ cup salad oil
1 lb. tomatoes, diced
1 lb. zucchini, cut in slices 1 inch thick

1 cup diced ham (optional)
2 ears fresh corn, cut into 2-inch pieces, or 1 can (1 lb.) kernel corn, drained
½ cup onion flakes
1 Tbs. chili powder
1 tsp. salt
1 clove garlic, minced

Combine flour, salt and black pepper in a paper bag. Add a few pieces of chicken at a time and shake; remove and repeat with rest of chicken. Heat oil in a large saucepan. Add chicken and brown on all sides. Drain excess fat. Add tomatoes, zucchini, ham (if used) and fresh corn. If using canned corn, add 15 minutes before stew is done. Combine onion flakes, chili powder, salt and minced garlic and blend into chicken mixture. Cover and simmer 1 hour or until chicken and vegetables are tender.

Makes 8 servings.

Chicken Fricassee with Almonds.

Pipián con Almendras y Pollo
Chicken Fricassee with Almonds

There are many varieties of *pipián*. This one is thickened and flavored with both sesame seeds and almonds.

2 Tbs. olive oil or salad oil
2 Tbs. lard
1 chicken (3 lb.) cut in serving-size pieces
¼ cup finely chopped onion
1 clove garlic, minced
1 chicken bouillon cube

1 cup boiling water
2 Tbs. lemon juice
2 tsp. chili powder
1 tsp. salt
½ tsp. oregano
½ cup almonds, ground
1 Tbs. sesame seeds
1 Tbs. chopped parsley

Place a large, dry skillet over moderate heat. Add sesame seeds and toast until lightly brown, about 2 minutes. Stir constantly. Remove from skillet and set aside. Heat oil and lard in skillet. Add chicken and brown well on all sides. Remove chicken and add onion and garlic. Stir until tender, not brown. Dissolve bouillon cube in 1 cup boiling water. Replace chicken in skillet and pour chicken broth over. Add lemon juice, chili powder, salt and oregano. Cover and reduce heat. Simmer about 25 minutes or until chicken is tender. Remove chicken to a serving platter and keep warm. Stir sesame seeds and ground almonds into skillet and simmer for 5 minutes. Spoon over chicken. Sprinkle with chopped parsley. Serve with plain boiled rice and a green vegetable.

Makes 4 to 5 servings.

Pollo Mexicano
Chicken Mexican Style

While chicken remains in the economy class, comparatively speaking, we welcome more recipes for serving it in attractive fashion. Here is another savory dish to borrow from those thrifty Mexican cooks.

3-lb. chicken
Gizzard from chicken
2 cups water
1 bay leaf

⅓ cup seedless raisins
⅓ cup sliced green olives

1¾	tsp. salt	⅓	cup sliced black
1	medium onion		olives
½	cup diced celery	¼	tsp. black pepper
¼	cup diced green	½	tsp. chili powder
	pepper	1	tsp. paprika
6	Tbs. tomato paste	1	large ripe avocado
			Pimiento

Wash and cut chicken in serving-size pieces. Place in a saucepan with gizzard, water, bay leaf, salt, onion, celery and green pepper. Cover and cook over low heat 1 hour or until chicken is tender. Add tomato paste, raisins, green and black olives, pepper, chili powder and paprika. Cook 5 minutes. Serve on a large platter. Peel and slice avocado and arrange over top of chicken. Garnish with pimiento cut in strips. Very good when served on a bed of cooked rice.

Makes 6 servings.

Ensalada de Pollo y Elote
Chicken and Corn Salad

A substantial main dish salad is always welcome, especially when the weather is sizzling or it's one of those busy, busy days. A gentle reminder: don't overcook the corn or it will toughen. A little bit of sugar in the cooking water will greatly increase the flavor!

6	ears fresh corn	¼	cup diced scallions
2	Tbs. fresh lemon	¼	cup chopped
	juice		parsley
6	Tbs. salad oil	2	cups diced cooked
1¼	tsp. salt		chicken
1¼	tsp. ground cumin		Lettuce
¼	tsp. pepper		

Cook corn in boiling water with about a teaspoon of sugar for 3 to 5 minutes, no longer. Drain and cool. Cut kernels from cob (makes about 4 cups). In a large bowl, combine oil, lemon juice, salt, cumin, black pepper, scallions and parsley. Add chicken and reserved corn. Toss well and serve on lettuce leaves.

Serves 6.

Meat 7

There's no need to serve the same old main dishes day after day when we can borrow some of the surefire successes from Mexican cooks. Proof that their food is highly appreciated by Americans who have been introduced to it is the large number of Mexican restaurants in every border town from Texas to California. The big complaint of many tourists who come back north is, in fact, "There isn't a decent Mexican restaurant in the whole town."

Mexican tastes have mingled so well that they have even given rise to a whole new style of cooking, known rather fondly as Tex-Mex. So, with perhaps some overtones of North American preferences, we can adopt new ideas, new taste treats to expand our own list of favorites and, incidentally, garner compliments from family and friends.

Cerdo de Durango
Durango Pork

This is an economical main dish to serve a hungry family and the answer to the end of a pork roast that isn't enough to go a second time around. In the latter case, just put it through your meat grinder and expand it with eggs in this fashion.

2 Tbs. salad oil	1 clove garlic, minced
1 lb. ground lean pork	Pinch cayenne pepper
¾ tsp. salt	1 tomato, diced
1 tsp. oregano	6 eggs, beaten

Heat oil in a large skillet. Add pork and cook, stirring constantly, until brown. Stir in seasonings and tomato. Cook, uncovered, over low heat 15 minutes, stirring occasionally. Pour beaten eggs over mixture and cook, stirring constantly, until eggs are set.

Makes 6 servings.

Cazuela de Carne
Meat Casserole

One of the nicest advantages of a main-dish casserole is that you can extend meat in a way that tastes very good and doesn't shortchange the family on nutritive value.

1½ lbs. ground beef	2 Tbs. chili powder
2 Tbs. salad oil	1 small onion, minced
1 can (1 lb., 12 oz.) tomatoes	1 tsp. salt
1 can (1 lb., 4 oz.) red kidney beans	½ tsp. pepper
¾ cup chopped, ripe olives	1 package (12 oz.) corn-muffin mix

Brown meat in hot oil. Add remaining ingredients except corn-muffin mix and blend well. Place in lightly greased 3-quart casserole. Bake in preheated slow oven (325°F.) 30 minutes. Prepare muffin mix according to package directions. Spoon mixture around edge of hot casserole, leaving an opening in the middle. Return to oven and increase temperature to 425° F. Bake an additional 25 minutes.

Makes 6 to 8 servings.

Chili Pork Stew from Puebla

½ cup dried chopped onion	1 tsp. oregano, crumbled
1½ tsp. instant minced garlic	⅛ tsp. sugar
1⅓ cups water, divided	2 lbs. potatoes, peeled and quartered
2 Tbs. oil	1 can (1 lb.) tomatoes, broken up
3 lbs. boneless pork shoulder, cut into 2-inch pieces	½ lb. *chorizo* or pork-sausage links, sliced
½ tsp. salt	1 avocado, peeled and sliced (optional)
3 Tbs. flour	
1 Tbs. chili powder	

Rehydrate chopped onion and garlic in ⅓ cup of the water for 10 minutes. In a large heavy saucepan or dutch oven, heat oil. Add pork; brown well on all sides. Remove pork; set aside. Drain all but 2 tablespoons fat from skillet. Add rehydrated onion and garlic; sauté 5 min-

Meat Casserole.

Chili Pork Stew from Puebla.

utes. Return pork to skillet. Add ¾ cup of the water along with the salt. Bring to boiling point. Cover and simmer 1½ hours or until pork is almost tender, stirring occasionally. Blend flour, chili powder, oregano and sugar with remaining ¼ cup water; stir into gravy in saucepan. Add potatoes, tomatoes and sausage. Cover and simmer until meat and potatoes are tender, about 40 to 45 minutes longer. Garnish with avocado slices, if desired.

Makes 8 servings

Chorizos y Frijoles
Sausage and Beans

While we're on an economy "kick," we might as well make our dishes taste good. This one will call for second helpings!

1 lb. bulk pork sausage	1 Tbs. salt
1 small onion, finely chopped	1 tsp. chili powder
	½ tsp. pepper
2 cups peeled, sliced tart apples	1 clove garlic, minced
1½ cups tomato juice	2 cans (1 lb. each) red kidney beans
1 Tbs. brown sugar	Sour cream (optional)

Combine sausage meat with remaining ingredients except sour cream and mix well. Place in large saucepan and simmer, uncovered, 15 to 20 minutes until most of liquid has evaporated. Serve hot, topped with sour cream if desired.

Makes 6 servings.

Fiesta Picadillo
Party Picadillo

Another savory recipe to make your ground meat go a long way! Serve with hot rice or tacos and you have a treat.

½ cup finely chopped onion	2 medium apples, peeled, cored and diced
1 clove finely chopped garlic	½ cup raisins
¼ cup salad oil, divided	½ cup sliced, stuffed olives
3 lbs. ground lean beef	1 Tbs. chili powder
1 can (1 lb., 12 oz.) tomatoes, broken up	2 tsp. salt
	1 can (4 oz.) blanched almonds, slivered

Cook onion and garlic in 3 tablespoons hot oil. Add beef, half at a time, and sauté until browned. Add tomatoes, apples, raisins, olives, chili powder and salt. Bring to boiling point. Reduce heat and simmer, uncovered, for 20 minutes, stirring occasionally. Heat remaining tablespoon oil in a small skillet and add almonds. Sauté for about 3 minutes or until lightly browned. Stir into beef mixture just before serving.

Makes 12 servings.

Sausage and Beans.

Party Picadillo.

Albóndigas en Salsa de Almendras
Meatballs in Almond Sauce

A delightful surprise for the family—tangy meatballs with hard-cooked eggs inside! They're nutritious and very good!

3 Tbs. olive or vegetable oil	1½ tsp. salt
½ small onion, minced	1 lb. ground lean beef
1 clove garlic, minced	1 large egg, beaten
⅔ cup finely chopped almonds	1 Tbs. chili powder
	Black pepper
2 cups soft bread crumbs	2 large, hard-cooked eggs
¼ cup tomato paste	Fat for frying
2 cups water	3 cups cooked rice
	Sliced, toasted almonds

Heat oil and stir in minced onion and garlic. Cook over moderate heat until tender but not brown. Add almonds, ⅔ cup bread crumbs and stir over low heat until crumbs are golden. Add tomato paste, water and salt and mix well.

Mix ground beef with beaten eggs, chili powder, pepper and remaining bread crumbs. Cut hard-cooked eggs in half lengthwise, then cut each half crosswise. Cover each piece of egg with meat mixture to make a 2-inch ball. Brown meatballs in hot fat, then add to the almond sauce, cover and simmer 15 minutes. Turn onto serving platter; place meatballs in center and surround with cooked rice. Garnish with toasted almonds.

Makes 6 servings.

Meatballs in Almond Sauce.

Carne Mexicana
Mexican Meat Loaf

2 eggs, lightly beaten	⅛ tsp. ground red pepper
1 can (8 oz.) tomato sauce	¼ tsp. instant minced garlic
½ cup instant minced onion	2½ lbs. ground meat-loaf mixture
¼ cup sweet pepper flakes	1 Tbs. melted butter
2 Tbs. chili powder	3 Tbs. dry bread crumbs
2 tsp. salt	

In a large mixing bowl combine eggs, tomato sauce, minced onion, pepper flakes, chili powder, salt, red pepper and minced garlic. Add meat; mix thoroughly, but do not overmix. Press into lightly buttered 9×5×3-inch loaf pan. Drizzle top with melted butter. Sprinkle with bread crumbs. Bake in a preheated hot oven (400°F.) 1 hour or until done. Let rest in pan 10 minutes before slicing.

Makes 8 servings.

Mexican Meat Loaf.

8
Chili con Carne

Chili con carne is not only a favorite dish on both sides of the Rio Grande, but there is a Chili Appreciation Society International. Its chili-loving members come from as far away as Australia, Japan and Vietnam. While chili con carne is more Texan than Mexican, there are chili con carne aficionados in Mexico City who can top the Texans when it comes to a taste for chili that throws long hot sparks.

Not only is chili powder the greatest for the esteemed chili con carne, but convenience-oriented homemakers use it in all kinds of meat, fish, fowl, egg or cheese dishes. Even though it is a nicely balanced blend as is, there's no law against stepping up any of the spices to your family's taste. Feel free to hot it up with red pepper, if you like. If your family adores garlic, add more of that. Extra cumin will make the dish taste more Latin American; oregano gives it a hint of an Italian accent.

When seasoning chili con carne, remember that if you want really fiery chili use 12 chili pepper pods or 12 tablespoons (¾ cup) chili powder per 3 pounds of meat. If you prefer it milder, cut the heat to 6 chili peppers or about ⅓ cup chili powder. The pods have been sun-dried and they are usually reddish. They give the bowl of chili its color as well as its WOW!

There are countless recipes for chili con carne. This one, seasoned with chili powder, is one of the best, especially when topped with a bit of sour cream.

Texas Jailhouse Chili

Because chili peppers and other spices made cheap cuts of beef so flavorful, bowls of chili con carne became standard on the menus of Texas jails, starting about eighty-five years ago. In fact, jails began to be judged by their chili recipes. There were wrongdoers who declared that the best chili of all was served in the Dallas County jail in the 1930s. Here is that recipe.

½ lb. ground beef suet
2 lbs. coarsely ground beef
3 garlic cloves, minced
1½ Tbs. paprika
3 Tbs. chili powder *or* 3 minced chili pepper pods

1 Tbs. ground cumin seed
1 Tbs. salt
1 tsp. ground white pepper
1½ Tbs. diced sweet pepper pods
3 cups water

Fry out the suet in a heavy kettle, then add the meat, garlic and other seasonings. Cook, covered, over low heat for 4 hours, stirring occasionally. Then add a little water, depending on how thick it is to be, and cook for another hour.

Makes 6 servings.

Barry Goldwater's Chili

Barry Goldwater is another distinguished chili cook. No two chili cooks use the same recipe, and this is the one used by the famous Arizonan. He uses paprika and red pepper as well as chili powder and adds chili beans, mushrooms and tomatoes. The senator sometimes serves chili cowboy style, that is, a cheeseburger on one slice of toast, the whole thing topped with chili con carne.

1 tsp. salt	1 can (15–16 oz.)
1 lb. ground round	beans in Mexican
steak	sauce
4 medium onions,	1 Tbs. sugar
chopped	1 Tbs. vinegar
1 can (4 oz.) mush-	2 tsp. chili powder
room stems and	Paprika, enough for
pieces	color
1 large can whole	Ground red pepper,
tomatoes	as desired

Sprinkle salt in heated skillet and brown in it the ground round steak and chopped onions, cooking the mixture until the meat is browned and the onions clear. Add mushroom stems and pieces, whole tomatoes, chili beans in Mexican sauce and remaining ingredients. Bring to boil, then lower heat and simmer for about an hour or until tomatoes cook down. Do not cover.

Makes 4 servings.

Pedernales River Chili

The late President Johnson, very much the Texan, used to say, "Chili concocted outside of Texas is usually a weak, apologetic imitation. . . . One of the first things I do when I go home is to have a bowl of red. There is simply nothing better." Here's how it would have been made.

4 lbs. of chili meat	2 Tbs. chili powder,
(course ground	or more if needed
meat)	Several dashes
1 large onion,	liquid hot pepper
chopped	sauce
2 cloves garlic,	1½ cups canned
minced	whole tomatoes
1 tsp. ground	Salt to taste
oregano	2 cups hot water
1 tsp. ground cumin	
seed	

Put meat, onions and garlic in large heavy skillet or dutch oven. Sear until gray colored. Add the oregano, cumin, chili powder, pepper sauce, tomatoes, salt and hot water. Bring to boil, lower heat and simmer covered, about 1 hour. As fat cooks out, skim.

Makes about 7 or 8 servings.

Nixon Chili

Former President Nixon started his chili con carne with uncooked beans and wanted about a quart of tomatoes in the batch.

1½ cups uncooked	3½ cups tomatoes
red chili beans	1 tsp. salt
Boiling water	1 to 3 tsp. chili
Salt	powder
1 lb. ground beef	1 or 2 cloves
1 large onion,	garlic, minced
chopped	1 tsp. paprika
1 green pepper,	Dash of cayenne
chopped	pepper
3 Tbs. fat	

Soak beans overnight in cold water. Cook in boiling salted water until tender. Drain well. Brown meat, onion and green pepper in hot fat. Add tomatoes and seasonings. Simmer slowly for 2 hours. Add water if necessary. Combine with beans and heat.

Makes 4 to 6 servings.

Eisenhower Chili con Carne

There are endless arguments about what should or should not go into chili con carne, and President Eisenhower was one of those who wanted beans in his bowl of chili, but no tomato. Here is his recipe as given in 1953. We question the amount of chili powder and suggest cutting it down to 2 or 3 tablespoons.

2 or 3 Tbs. bacon grease	1 Tbs. salt
6 to 8 medium-sized onions	2 oz. chili powder
	1½ quarts hot water
1 or 2 cloves garlic, minced	3 cans chili beans
	1 heaping tsp. ground cumin
2 lbs. ground round steak or chuck (not too fat)	Flour paste to thicken

In a large skillet or dutch oven, heat the bacon grease, add chopped onions and garlic. Cook slowly about 10 minutes, stirring occasionally, then add the ground meat. When the meat has lost its red color, add salt and chili powder, stir well and add water. Cook slowly for about 45 minutes to an hour. Add beans and cumin and thicken with flour and water to proper consistency. Cook several hours before it is to be served, then reheat. Or, better still, make it a day beforehand and then reheat.

Makes 6 to 8 servings.

Havasu Chili con Carne

Among this country's great chili con carne cooks is C. V. Wood, Jr., the tycoon who had London Bridge moved, stone by stone, from England to Lake Havasu City, Arizona. The ingredient list of his prize-winning dish goes on and on and on. But it's good!

3 lbs. flank steak	2 tsp. oregano
5 lbs. thinly sliced pork chops	2 tsp. ground cumin seed
2-lb. stewing chicken	3 Tbs. ground black pepper
Water	3 Tbs. chili powder
4 or 5 medium tomatoes, peeled and chopped	2 cloves garlic, minced
¼ cup minced celery	1 cup chopped onion
¼ cup minced onion	1 cup chopped green pepper
Salt, pepper to taste	1 lb. shredded Monterey Jack cheese
5 or 6 long green chilies, seared, peeled and chopped	Juice of 1 lime

Trim all fat from flank steak and cut meat into ⅜-inch cubes. Remove center part from pork chops and discard all fat and bones. Stew chicken 2 to 3 hours in about 6 cups water. Reserve 1 quart broth and set chicken aside for another use. Combine tomatoes, celery, ¼ cup onion, salt and pepper to taste, and cook 3 hours, adding enough water to yield 1 quart sauce. In a 6-quart pot combine steak, pork, chicken broth, tomato sauce, chilies, oregano, cumin, black pepper, chili powder, garlic and salt to taste. Simmer 1 hour. Add 1 cup onion and green pepper and cook 2 hours longer. Meat should be coming apart in shreds. If not, cook another 30 minutes. During the last 5 minutes of cooking time, stir in cheese and lime juice. Serve at once.

Makes 12 to 15 servings.

Chili con Carne with Beef and Ham

½ cup onion flakes	1½ to 3 Tbs. chili powder
½ tsp. instant minced garlic	1 tsp. salt
⅓ cup water	1 can (1 lb., 4 oz.) kidney beans
3 Tbs. oil	
1½ lbs. beef round steak	¼ cup beef broth, red wine or water, if needed
1 lb. ham steak	
1 can (1 lb.) tomatoes, broken up	Sour cream, if desired

Chili con Carne with Beef and Ham.

Mix onion flakes and minced garlic with water; let stand 10 minutes to soften. Heat oil in a large skillet. Add softened onion and garlic; sauté until golden. Dice steak into ½-inch cubes. Add to skillet and cook until brown. Add tomatoes, chili powder and salt. Bring to boiling point; reduce heat and simmer, uncovered, stirring occasionally, for 1 hour. Stir in kidney beans and simmer ½ hour longer. If necessary, thin mixture with broth, wine or water. Top with a large dollop of sour cream, if desired.

Makes 6 to 8 servings.

Chicken with Chili I

1 Tbs. instant minced onion	2 Tbs. minced parsley
1 Tbs. sweet pepper flakes	4 tsp. chili powder
2 Tbs. water	1 tsp. salt
1 Tbs. oil	1 tsp. oregano leaves, crumbled
1 lb. ground lean beef	½ tsp. sugar
1 can (1 lb.) tomatoes, broken up	3½ cups cooked rice
	4 cups cooked chicken chunks
1 can (6 oz.) tomato paste	1 cup shredded Monterey Jack or Cheddar cheese

Rehydrate onion and pepper flakes in water for 10 minutes. In a large skillet heat oil. Add beef; brown, about 5 minutes, stirring to break up meat. Add rehydrated onion and pepper flakes, tomatoes, tomato paste, parsley, chili powder, salt, oregano and sugar. Bring to boiling point. Reduce heat and simmer, uncovered, for 5 minutes. In a 12×8×2-inch casserole arrange a layer of meat sauce, a layer of rice and a layer of chicken. Repeat layering once more. Sprinkle with cheese. Bake in a preheated moderate oven (375°F.) until bubbly and cheese melts, about 30 minutes. Let stand 10 minutes before serving.

Makes 8 servings.

Chicken with Chili II

2 Tbs. oil	1 can (1 lb., 4 oz.) red kidney beans
½ cup finely minced onion	
1 clove garlic, minced	2 cups diced cooked chicken
1 can (1 lb.) tomatoes, broken up	1 package (12 oz.) corn-muffin mix
½ green pepper, diced	1 Tbs. chopped parsley
2 Tbs. chili powder	1 egg
1¼ tsp. salt	⅔ cup milk
Freshly ground black pepper	

Heat oil in large skillet and cook minced onion and garlic until tender. Add tomatoes, green pepper, chili powder, salt and black pepper. Simmer, uncovered, stirring occasionally. Add kidney beans and chicken. Turn into a 3-quart casserole; set aside. In a small mixing bowl combine muffin mix with parsley. Stir in egg and milk and mix only until blended. Spoon batter around outer edge of casserole. Bake in a preheated hot oven (425°F.) 20 to 25 minutes or until topping is nicely browned.

Makes 6 servings.

Queso con Chili
Cheese with Chili

Chili but hot, a nutritious supper dish that's easy and full of flavor!

1 lb. sharp American or Cheddar cheese	1½ tsp. chili powder
	1 large egg
⅓ cup butter	¼ tsp. salt
¼ cup warm milk	Hot toast or crackers

Dice cheese and place in top part of double boiler with butter. Stir over hot, not boiling, water until cheese has melted. Stir in milk and chili powder and continue until mixture is smooth. Beat in egg and salt. Cook slowly 1 minute. Serve over hot toast or crackers.

Makes 6 servings.

9
Vegetables

Frijoles Refritos
Refried Beans

Instead of potatoes *every* day, you'll enjoy going Mexican once in a while with economical, delicious refried beans. A great favorite in Mexico when served as a vegetable or as a filling for tacos.

¼ cup instant minced onion
1 tsp. instant minced garlic
¼ cup water
2 Tbs. bacon fat or lard
1 can (1 lb., 4 oz.) red kidney beans, well drained and mashed

2 Tbs. tomato paste
1½ tsp. chili powder
½ tsp. oregano leaves, crumbled
½ tsp. salt
½ cup grated sharp Cheddar cheese

Mix minced onion and garlic in water; let stand 10 minutes to rehydrate. In a medium skillet heat bacon fat. Add rehydrated onion and garlic and sauté 5 minutes, stirring constantly. Stir in beans; cook until dry. Add tomato paste, chili powder, oregano, salt; mix well. Add cheese and cook only until hot and cheese begins to melt.

Makes 3 to 4 servings.

Frijoles Refritos   II

5 Tbs. lard
2 medium onions, finely chopped
2 cloves garlic, minced
1 tsp. salt
⅛ tsp. pepper

1 bay leaf
1 tsp. chili powder
½ cup canned tomatoes, drained
1 can (15½ oz.) red kidney beans

Heat 3 tablespoons lard in a 2-quart saucepan and add chopped onion. Stir constantly with a wooden spoon until onion is soft but not brown. Add minced garlic and salt and continue to stir over medium heat for 3 minutes. Add remaining ingredients and heat through. Remove bay leaf, then mash mixture with a wooden spoon. Heat remaining 2 tablespoons lard in a 9-inch skillet. Add bean mixture and stir until it is hot and creamy.

Makes 6 servings.

Tip: While it may not be the Mexican way of doing things, you might prefer to blend all the ingredients in a blender (except the bay leaf) and then reheat in the 2 tablespoons of hot lard.

Frijoles con Queso I
Kidney Beans with Cheese

While the Mexicans do not eat as much meat as we do, they add protein to their diet with the lavish use of beans. When combined with cheese, the result is an economical and nutritious dish with a tantalizing flavor that is very easy to prepare.

1 can (15½ oz.) red   1 small onion,
   kidney beans   minced
1 cup grated Romano   1 Tbs. green pepper
   or Parmesan   Few grains cayenne
   cheese   pepper

Blend all ingredients together in a saucepan. Stir over moderate heat with a wooden spoon. Serve when hot.

Makes 4 to 6 servings.

Kidney Beans with Cheese.

Tip: You may prefer to substitute other canned beans available in the supermarket. *Garbanzos* (chick peas), for instance, will do very nicely.

Frijoles con Queso II

An inexpensive main dish that tastes good too!

¼ cup finely minced   ½ cup tomato sauce
   onion   4 tsp. chili powder
¼ cup finely diced   1 tbs. chopped
   green pepper   parsley
3 slices bacon   1½ tsp. oregano
1 can (1 lb.) to-   1 tsp. salt
   matoes, broken up   Pepper to taste
1 can (1 lb. 4 oz.)   ¼ lb. sharp Cheddar
   red kidney beans   cheese, grated

Combine minced onion and green pepper. Cook bacon in skillet until crisp. Remove from skillet, crumble and set aside. Add onion and green pepper to fat in skillet and sauté about 4 minutes. Add tomatoes, half the kidney beans, tomato sauce, chili powder, parsley, oregano, salt and pepper. Mix well. Mash remaining half of kidney beans and stir into mixture. Cook, covered, 15 minutes or until sauce has thickened, stirring ocasionally. Blend in cheese and stir until melted. Serve with cooked rice if desired.

Makes 6 servings.

Zanahorias con Cumino
Diced Carrots with Cumin

Not like plain vegetables—and very tempting when the right spice is added.

14 small young car-   ½ tsp. ground cumin
   rots   seeds
   1 tsp. salt   1/16 tsp. ground black
   1 Tbs. butter   pepper
   1 Tbs. flour   1 Tbs. minced
         parsley

Wash, scrape and dice carrots. Run 1 inch depth of water into saucepan. Add salt and bring to boiling point. Cook carrots 10 minutes or until crisp but tender. Drain water into measuring cup and set aside. Melt butter in saucepan. Blend in flour and cumin. Stir and cook until lightly browned. Remove from heat and gradually stir in carrot water, adding more water to make 1 cup if necessary. Cook until slightly thickened. Stir in carrots, black pepper and parsley. Serve at once.

Makes 6 servings.

Maíz Mexicano
Mexican Corn Sauté

Corn in any fashion appeals to Mexicans. This is a specially good recipe.

6 ears fresh corn	3 tomatoes, peeled
2 Tbs. salad oil	and diced
1 cup chopped	1½ tsp. salt
onion	½ tsp. ground cumin
1 cup chopped	¼ tsp. sugar
green pepper	1/16 tsp. ground red
½ tsp. finely minced	pepper
garlic	

Remove husks and silks from corn. Cut kernels off the cobs (to make about 3½ cups) and set aside. In a large skillet heat oil. Add onion, green pepper and garlic; sauté 8 minutes over moderate heat, stirring constantly. Stir in reserved corn; sauté 3 minutes. Add remaining ingredients and cook 8 minutes longer, stirring occasionally.

Makes 6 to 8 servings.

Maíz y Calabaza Mexicanos
Mexican Corn and Zucchini

A delightful and unusual combination.

2 Tbs. bacon fat	1½ tsp. salt
2 cups corn, cut	½ tsp. sugar
from cob	½ tsp. ground cumin
2 cups diced fresh	seed
tomatoes	⅛ tsp. ground black
2 cups sliced	pepper
zucchini squash	

Heat fat in 10-inch skillet or saucepan. Add vegetables and seasonings. Cover and cook 10 minutes or until vegetables are just tender. Serve hot, garnished with strips of pimiento, if desired.

Makes approximately 8 servings.

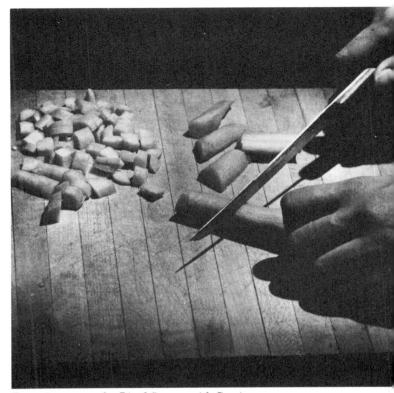

Preparing carrots for Diced Carrots with Cumin.

Mexican Corn Sauté.

Frituras de Cebolla con Yerbas
Onion Fritters

Another imaginative way to dress up a lowly vegetable.

1 cup flour	1 egg, well beaten
1 tsp. baking powder	⅔ cup water
½ tsp. salt	3 medium-sized
½ tsp. chili powder	onions (¾ lb.)
1 tsp. sugar	Fat for deep frying

Sift together flour, baking powder, salt, chili powder and sugar. Blend egg with water and add. Beat to make a smooth batter. Peel onions and cut into crosswise slices ¼ inch thick. Add salt. Mix well. Dip onion slices into batter and fry in deep fat preheated to 360°F. until they are browned and float to the top of the fat. Drain on paper towels. Serve hot.

Makes 4 servings.

Rellenos de Plátanos Maduros
Stuffed Plantains

Many of us aren't familiar with plantains; they look like big green bananas! So in the event your market doesn't carry them, you can settle for unripe bananas with a decided greenish tinge.

Plantains.

3 firm plantains or	Flour
unripe bananas	1 large egg, beaten
Oil	Bread crumbs
Meat stuffing (recipe following)	

Remove skins and slice each plantain in half lengthwise. In a large skillet, pour oil to a depth of ⅛ inch and heat. Add a few slices of plantain at a time and fry on both sides until golden. Remove and drain on paper towels. Bend each slice into a circle and fasten with toothpicks. Fill with meat stuffing and then refrigerate for at least 4 hours. Dip stuffed plantains into flour, then beaten egg and finally into bread crumbs. Fry one side until golden, turn and repeat for second side.

Makes 6 servings.

Meat stuffing

½ small onion, minced	1¼ tsp. salt
	¼ tsp. pepper
½ green bell pepper, minced	½ tsp. oregano
	1 clove garlic,
2 Tbs. oil	minced
1 lb. ground, lean beef	¼ cup soft bread crumbs
1½ tsp. capers	1 large egg, beaten

Sauté onion and pepper in hot oil until tender. Add meat, capers, salt, pepper, oregano and garlic and stir until meat is brown. Cool slightly. Blend in bread crumbs and egg and mix well; chill thoroughly. Use to stuff prepared plantains.

Chilies Rellenos
Stuffed Peppers

In Mexico the visitor often finds chilies stuffed with meat, seafood or cheese, but in the United States cheese seems to be the favorite. Be sure to use the California green chili for this and not our regular fresh green pepper.

1 can (7 oz.)	½ cup flour
California green	Salad oil for frying
chili peppers	Tomato sauce (optional)
½ lb. sharp Cheddar cheese	
Batter (recipe follows)	Sliced scallion tops for garnish (optional)

Two typical market scenes from Guadalajara.

Drain chilies, rinse and cut a slit in the side of each. Being careful not to tear, gently remove seeds and white pith (called "veins" in Mexico). Cut cheese into strips ½ inch wide, ½ inch deep and 1 inch shorter than the chili. Fill each pepper with cheese. Prepare batter as instructed below. Just before frying, roll each stuffed chili in flour and then shake off excess lightly. This helps the batter to coat the chili.

Pour salad oil to a depth of about ¼ inch in a large skillet. When oil is hot, dip chilies in batter and immediately place in oil. Dip just as many as you can handle at one time. When chilies are brown on one side, turn with a fork or spatula to brown other side. When golden brown all over, remove and place on paper towels. May be served with hot tomato sauce and garnished with scallions. Serve hot.

Makes about 4 servings.

Batter for crisp coating

5 large eggs, separated
1 tsp. salt

Beat yolks until thick and lemon colored. Add salt to whites and beat until peaks form when beater is lifted. Carefully blend a small amount into the yolks and then add remainder, using a folding motion. Mixture is now ready to coat the chilies.

Chili Cheese-Stuffed Potatoes

6 large baking potatoes	1 Tbs. milk
½ cup shredded Monterey Jack or Cheddar cheese	1 tsp. chili powder
	¾ tsp. salt
	⅛ tsp. ground black pepper
¼ cup butter	

Bake potatoes in a preheated oven (400°F.) 1 hour and 15 minutes or until done. Remove from oven and cut each potato in half lengthwise. With a spoon scoop out potato, leaving the shells intact. Mash potato until fluffy with the remaining ingredients. Spoon into potato shells. Place under preheated hot broiler until well flecked with brown.

Makes 6 servings.

Cazuela de Calabaza
Spiced Pumpkin Casserole

Another popular squash is served up with imagination and seasonings.

4 cups cooked mashed pumpkin	¼ tsp. ground cinnamon
¼ cup brown sugar	1 tsp. grated lemon rind
½ tsp. salt	
⅛ tsp. ground black pepper	1 tsp. grated orange rind
¼ tsp. ground nutmeg	¼ cup butter, melted
½ tsp. ground ginger	

Combine all ingredients thoroughly and place in buttered 1-quart casserole. Bake in a preheated moderate oven (350°F.) 1 hour or until hot and the top is golden brown. Serve with ham, pork or poultry.

Makes 6 servings.

Espinaca Deliciosa
Savory Spinach

Because it's so perishable, spinach doesn't thrive in hot weather, but when the Mexicans can get it, they do wonders.

The ingredients for Chilies Rellenos.

2 lbs. fresh spinach
2 Tbs. butter
½ cup minced onion
½ tsp. crumbled oregano
½ tsp. sugar
1¼ tsp. salt
⅛ tsp. garlic powder
⅛ tsp. ground black pepper
1 tsp. fresh lemon juice
3 Tbs. grated Monterey Jack or Cheddar cheese
Onion rings

Wash spinach and place in a saucepan with only the water that clings to the leaves. Cover and cook about 5 minutes or until spinach is wilted and tender. Remove from heat and cut crisscross with 2 sharp knives. Drain if necessary. Heat butter in saucepan. Add minced onion and sauté until limp, about 3 minutes. Add seasonings and lemon juice. Pour over spinach. Toss lightly. Turn into serving dish. Sprinkle with grated cheese. Garnish with paper-thin onion rings, if desired.

Makes 5 or 6 servings.

Batata Rumba
Sweet Potato Rhumba

A rather frivolous title for an extragood dish.

4 cups hot, boiled, mashed sweet potatoes
¼ cup butter
⅓ cup heavy cream
½ tsp. ground nutmeg
½ tsp. salt
¼ cup brown sugar
2 Tbs. rum
1 Tbs. butter, melted
1 Tbs. grated orange peel

Combine all ingredients except 1 tablespoon butter and orange peel, using enough cream to make mixture fluffy. Place mixture in 1-quart buttered casserole. Drizzle top with melted butter and sprinkle with grated orange peel. Bake in preheated hot oven (400°F.) for 35 minutes or until top is brown.

Makes 6 to 8 servings.

Chili Cheese-Stuffed Potatoes.

Savory Spinach.

Plátanos y Batatas
Bananas and Sweet Potato
They make a delicious twosome.

3 cups cold, cooked, mashed sweet potatoes	½ tsp. ground nutmeg
3 bananas, mashed	¼ tsp. salt
1 Tbs. lemon juice	⅛ tsp. ground black pepper
3 Tbs. butter	⅓ cup undiluted evaporated milk
⅓ cup light brown sugar	3 eggs, beaten

Make sure the sweet potatoes are cold, to prevent browning the bananas. Mix all ingredients thoroughly and place in buttered 1-quart casserole. Place in a pan of hot water. Bake in a preheated moderate oven (350°F.) 1 hour or until mixture is puffed and browned. Serve with poultry or ham.

Makes 6 servings.

Calabaza Mexicana
Zucchini Mexican Style
An unusual and delicious way of serving zucchini.

4 medium (1½ lb.) fresh tomatoes	1/16 tsp. garlic powder
2 Tbs. minced onion	8 medium small (2¼ lb.) unpeeled zucchini squash
½ cup minced celery	
½ tsp. basil	
⅓ cup olive oil	Flour
1 Tbs. capers	3 large hard-cooked eggs
1½ tsp. salt	
¼ tsp. ground black pepper	¼ cup minced parsley

Combine tomatoes, onion and celery. Cover and cook slowly 20 minutes or until vegetables are soft. Force through coarse sieve or whirl in blender. Add basil and olive oil. Cook 10 minutes or until thickened. Stir in capers, salt, black pepper and garlic powder. Set aside while preparing squash. Wash zucchini and cut, unpeeled, into lengthwise slices ¼ inch thick. Sprinkle with flour. Cook slowly in olive oil until lightly browned on both sides. Remove to serving platter. Spoon the warm tomato sauce over the top. Chop hard-cooked eggs finely, mix with parsley and sprinkle over top.

Makes 8 servings.

Stuffed Small Squashes
"Calabazitas" is the very pretty name for small squashes that are favorite Mexican vegetables. Chose yellow or white summer squash or zucchini for this dish.

4 small squashes	1 tsp. salt
2 Tbs. minced onion	¼ tsp. ground black pepper
2 Tbs. butter	
2 hard-cooked eggs, chopped	⅓ cup soft bread crumbs
½ cup grated sharp Cheddar cheese	¼ cup butter
	½ cup boiling water
2 raw eggs, beaten	

Wash and cut squash in half lengthwise. Remove seeds and stringy portions. Scoop out meat of squash and chop fine. Sauté onion in butter. Add squash pulp, hard-cooked eggs, cheese, raw eggs, salt and black pepper and pile into squash shells. Sprinkle with bread crumbs. Dot with butter. Place in an 8×12×2-inch baking pan. Pour in the ½ cup boiling water. Bake in a preheated moderate oven (375°F.) for 30 minutes or until crumbs are brown and mixture is set.

Makes 4 servings.

Bananas and Sweet Potato.

10
Sauces and Salads

Sauces have been very much a part of the Mexican kitchen from well before the time of the Spanish conquest. We know from descriptions of the historians during the era of the *conquistadores* that the Indians made good use of native ingredients. Tomatoes, chilies and avocados were combined with herbs and seasonings to make a fascinating assortment of sauces, varying from mild to pungent to very hot. One of the modern sauces is even labeled *"Esta sí pica,"* which can be translated as "This one really stings"—and so it does!

Whenever you buy a Mexican chili sauce, you may be sure it's hot, something like our own Tabasco sauce. Apart from the sauces that belong to individual dishes such as the *mole* in *Mole de Guajolote* (Turkey with Sauce), there are various sauces that go on the dining room table automatically along with salt and pepper. You may very well find a bottle of *salsa cruda* (uncooked tomato sauce) or *salsa verde* (green sauce), both of them freshly made. These are often added by the individual·diner to liven up a "dry" soup, meat or fish that may be unadorned, or they may be poured on a tortilla before rolling it up and so turning it into a taco.

Fresh *guacamole,* made whenever avocados are in season, is used as a sauce to accompany other foods, as a cocktail dip or as part of a salad. Many of the bottled sauces can be purchased in Spanish-American stores, but if you have a delicate mouth, be selective in your choice.

Salsa de Jitomate
Tomato Sauce

In these days of high food prices, many of us are growing our own vegetables. To every amateur gardener, however, there comes a time when we wonder what to do with all the tomatoes that seem to ripen at the same time. Here are some flavorful ways of using them on days when we don't feel like canning.

2 Tbs. salad oil
1 medium onion, finely chopped
2 cloves garlic, minced
2 large, ripe tomatoes, peeled, seeded and chopped
1 teaspoon sugar

2 canned *serrano* chilies, chopped, *or* 2 green Italian peppers
Salt and freshly ground pepper to taste
1 Tbs. fresh coriander, if available

Heat oil in skillet and cook onion until it is tender but not brown. Add minced garlic and cook 1 more minute. Add remaining ingredients except coriander and stir over moderate heat for 15 minutes. Correct seasoning. Add coriander, if used, and stir for 2 more minutes. Remove coriander before serving. This sauce can be served either hot or cold.

Makes approximately 2 cups.

Tip: To peel tomatoes, drop one at a time into a pan of water at full, rolling boil. If tomatoes are very ripe and thin skinned, they only need to be left about 10 seconds in the water. The thick-skinned variety may need as much as a minute. The skin should then separate easily. To seed, cut tomato in half (be sure to wash and dry your knife immediately to avoid stains), then squeeze very gently. Seeds will come out without any difficulty.

Salsa Cruda
Uncooked Tomato Sauce

This sauce is a great favorite on the Mexican table. Try it with hot or cold meats, poultry and fish when they are served without their own sauce, scrambled eggs and omelets and as a filling in tacos and tostados. It's a versatile condiment.

2 large, very ripe tomatoes, peeled and finely chopped	1 Tbs. fresh coriander or parsley, chopped
2 canned *serrano* chilies, chopped	Salt and pepper to taste
1 medium onion, finely chopped	¼ tsp. sugar

Blend all ingredients well and correct seasoning. Chill before serving.

Makes approximately 2½ cups of sauce.

Salsa Ranchera
Country Style Sauce

If you are unable to get the canned *jalapeño* chilies, try substituting 2 pale-green Italian peppers with 2 teaspoons chili powder.

2 Tbs. salad oil	Salt and pepper to taste
2 large tomatoes, peeled, seeded and cut in very small pieces	¼ tsp. sugar
	1 can (12 oz.) *jalapeño* chilies rinsed and chopped
	1 Tbs. lemon juice

Heat oil in skillet, add tomatoes and stir over moderate heat to a thick pulp. Add seasoning to taste and sugar. Remove from heat and add chilies (or peppers), which have been sautéed and chopped (together with chili powder, if used). Add lemon juice and mix well. Serve hot.

Makes approximately 1½ cups sauce.

Salsa de Almendras
Almond Sauce

This is a very good sauce to serve with tongue or veal. It may be served hot or cold.

2 Tbs. lard	¼ tsp. powdered cloves
½ cup blanched almonds	Salt and pepper to taste
1 slice stale bread	
2 green tomatoes, peeled and seeded	2 cups beef or chicken stock
½ medium onion, chopped	2 Tbs. vinegar
2 cloves garlic	1 tsp. sugar

Melt lard in large skillet. When hot, add blanched almonds and stir over moderate heat until they are lightly browned. Remove with slotted spoon and drain on paper towels. Add bread to skillet, adding more lard if necessary, and brown on both sides. Peel and seed tomatoes. Cut up and place in electric blender with almonds, fried bread (broken up), onion, garlic, powdered cloves, salt and pepper. Blend until mixture is smooth. Return mixture to skillet and stir over moderate heat for 5 minutes. Add stock, vinegar and sugar and cook until thick.

Makes approximately 2½ cups sauce.

Salsa Verde
Green Sauce

Made with readily available ingredients, this attractively colored sauce is good with fish or cold meats.

3 large onions, canned or boiled until tender
1 bunch parsley
1 slice white bread, soaked in 2 Tbs. vinegar
2 cups hot water
Salt and pepper to taste
3 Tbs. olive oil
3 cloves garlic

Cut up onions in small pieces and place in electric blender with remaining ingredients. Blend until thoroughly combined. Pour into saucepan (not aluminum) and stir over moderate heat until mixture thickens. Serve hot.

Makes approximately 2½ to 3 cups of sauce.

Salsa de Chili Rojo
Red Chili Sauce

This is the classic Mexican red chili sauce. It's fairly mild, but if your taste runs to something more fiery, try crumbling one of the dried red chilies and adding to the mixture. *Always* wash your hands immediately after handling a hot chili. If you should absentmindedly rub your eyes after touching it, there'd be trouble!

4 canned *ancho* chilies
2 large ripe tomatoes, peeled, seeded and chopped
1 large onion, chopped
2 cloves garlic
2 sprigs parsley
Salt and freshly ground pepper
½ tsp. sugar
¼ cup olive oil
2 Tbs. wine vinegar

Rinse canned chilies and place in blender with tomatoes, chopped, onion and garlic, parsley, salt, pepper and sugar. Heat in a saucepan (not aluminum) and stir constantly for 5 minutes. Cool, then stir in olive oil and vinegar. Can be placed on the table to use with "dry" soups, meat, fish or tortillas.

Makes about 2 cups.

Ensalada de César
Caesar Salad

Did you know that the famous Caesar Salad was created in Tijuana, Mexico? Its originator, Caesar Cardini, a Beverly Hills food specialist, was on duty in a Mexican restaurant one Fourth

Green Sauce is easily made in a blender.

The famous caesar salad.

of July many years ago when he suddenly ran out of supplies for his guests. After scouring the pantry, he managed to gather together some eggs, romaine lettuce, stale bread and Romanello cheese. This enterprising chef coddled the eggs and stirred them into a pear-wine vinegar and oil dressing, soaked the bread in olive oil, grated the cheese and tossed them all together in a garlic-rubbed salad bowl, along with a handful of croutons.

Named by the International Society of Epicures in Paris as "the greatest original dish to come out of the United States in the last 50 years," Ceasar Salad is Mexican by birth, American by adoption.

As with many traditional dishes, inventive cooks have added their own touch, and Caesar Salad is no exception. A purist may want to omit the mustard and anchovies, but many people think they add zing.

3 Tbs. butter	3 Tbs. olive oil
2 cloves garlic, crushed	2 Tbs. lemon juice
	¾ tsp. salt
2 cups small bread cubes	¼ tsp. black pepper (freshly ground)
¼ tsp. powdered mustard	1 large egg
	½ cup grated Parmesan cheese
¼ tsp. warm water	
1 head romaine lettuce	3 anchovy fillets, diced

In a small skillet melt butter; stir in crushed garlic. Add bread cubes and sauté until golden; set aside. In a cup combine mustard with water; let stand 10 minutes for flavor to develop. Tear lettuce into bite-sized pieces and place in a large salad bowl. Combine mustard with olive oil, lemon juice, salt and pepper; mix well. Pour over lettuce. Break egg into center of salad. Toss well. Add sautéed bread cubes, cheese and anchovies. Toss gently and serve immediately.

Makes 8 servings.

Ensalada de Aguacate Relleno con Salsa Francesa de Menta
Stuffed Avocado Salad with
Mint French Dressing

This salad has a long name, but it's also long on flavor and eye appeal! Refreshing as a salad after the main course and equally good served California style, before the entrée.

3 ripe avocados	½ cup toasted, shredded coconut
½ cup seedless grapes or other grapes, halved and seeded	Red or green Maraschino cherries
1½ cups fresh pine-apple, cut in cubes, or 1 package frozen pineapple cubes, partially defrosted	Lettuce

Scoop out avocado halves with French ball cutter or teaspoon. Combine with grapes and pineapple. Marinate in mint french dressing for 1 hour. Drain and divide into avocado shells. Top with toasted coconut and cherries; then arrange each shell on a bed of lettuce.

Makes 6 servings.

Mint French Dressing

½ tsp. salt	6 Tbs. olive or other oil
¼ tsp. dry mustard	
Dash cayenne pepper	2 Tbs. lemon juice or vinegar
1 tsp. tomato paste	4 sprigs fresh mint

Blend all ingredients well, breaking up mint leaves to extract more flavor. Let stand at room temperature 1 hour before using.

Enough to dress 6 servings of salad.

Ensalada de Ejotes
Green Bean Salad

Too often vegetables become the stepchild of the menu. For the most part they are over-cooked and come to the table a soggy mess. They lose not only their nutritive value but much of the flavor too! Yet it's easy to cook them correctly, and what a world of difference in the texture and flavor!

1 lb. fresh snap beans	1 tsp. salt
½ inch boiling water	¼ tsp. ground black pepper

1 tsp. salt	2 Tbs. minced onion
2 Tbs. salad or olive oil	Shredded lettuce
2 Tbs. fresh lemon juice	Shredded Muenster cheese

Cut tips from snap beans and cut into lengthwise halves. Place in saucepan with ½ inch boiling water and 1 teaspoon salt. Bring to boiling point in uncovered saucepan, then cover and cook *only* until crisp but tender, about 12 to 15 minutes. Drain if necessary. Cool and chill. Add oil, lemon juice, salt, pepper and onion. Toss lightly. Serve on shredded lettuce. Sprinkle with grated cheese.

Makes 6 to 8 servings.

Aguacates Rellenos I
Stuffed Avocados

Aguacate is a familiar name on restaurant menus in Mexico, for the avocado lends itself well to a variety of fillings. Following are a few of the favorites to serve either as an appetizer or salad.

2 large potatoes, boiled and cubed	1 rib celery, finely chopped
1 cup cooked string beans, coarsely chopped	¼ cup French dressing
	3 avocados
	Lettuce
	¼ cup mayonnaise

Marinate potatoes, string beans and celery in French dressing for 20 to 30 minutes. Peel avocados just before serving and cut in half lengthwise. Place on lettuce served in individual plates. Drain vegetables and divide into avocado halves. Serve with mayonnaise.

Makes 6 servings.

Aguacates Rellenos II
Stuffed Avocados

½ cup minced celery	½ cup toasted almond slivers
2 red apples, cored and diced	3 avocados
½ cup French dressing	Lettuce
	¼ cup mayonnaise

Green Bean Salad.

Avocado stuffed with vegetables.

To blanch almonds, place in a small bowl and pour boiling water over to cover. Let stand 3 minutes, then drain and cover with cold water. Skins then slip off easily. Pat dry with paper towels and cut in slivers lengthwise. Since toasted almonds have a much more definite flavor than almonds left "as is," place them in a shallow pan and heat in a moderate oven (350°F.) until golden brown, shaking the pan occasionally to turn them.

Blend celery with diced apples (leave skin on apples for added color). Marinate in French dressing for 20 to 30 minutes. Drain and mix with almond slivers. Peel avocados and cut in half lengthwise. Arrange on lettuce leaves on individual plates and fill with almond mixture. Serve with mayonnaise.

Makes 6 servings.

Aguacates Rellenos III
Stuffed Avocados

½ lb. cooked shrimp	½ cup mayonnaise
2 ribs celery, finely chopped	3 avocados
½ green bell pepper, finely chopped	Lettuce

To cook shrimp, place in a saucepan with enough boiling water to cover, along with a bay leaf, 3 or 4 peppercorns and a tablespoon of vinegar. Reduce heat to a simmer, for shrimp should never be allowed to boil. High heat toughens them so that you will think you're chewing on rubber. Let cook just long enough for the shrimp to turn pink and the flesh opaque—about 3 minutes for fresh shrimp and 5 or 6 minutes for the frozen type. Turn off heat and let shrimp cool in the liquid before shelling and deveining them.

Cut shrimp in half lengthwise and blend with celery, green pepper and mayonnaise. Cut avocados in half but do not remove skin. Fill each cavity with shrimp mixture and place on lettuce arranged on individual plates.

If you have any leftover beer around, you can use it for the cooking liquid instead of water; it adds an interesting flavor.

Makes 6 servings.

Ensalada de Garbanzos
Chick Pea Salad

Salads must offer a variety of color and shape to be attractive. You can add interest to this chick pea salad by slicing the carrots on a rather long, diagonal slant rather than straight across. It's a tip from the Chinese, who are artists with their food arrangements.

2 cups cooked or canned chick peas (*garbanzos*)	12 stuffed olives
	3 carrots, peeled and sliced
¼ cup French dressing	3 hard-cooked eggs, sliced
Lettuce	½ cup mayonnaise

Let chick peas (*garbanzos*) marinate in French dressing at least 1 hour. Drain and place in salad bowl lined with lettuce. Garnish with olives, carrots and hard-cooked egg slices. Serve with mayonnaise.

Makes 6 servings.

Avocado stuffed with shrimp.

Chick Pea Salad.

11
Desserts

Rosca de Reyes
Three Kings Coffee Cake

A delicious coffee cake, traditionally served in early January but enjoyable all year round.

2 packages active dry yeast
¼ cup warm water (110° to 115° F.)
1 cup milk
6½ cups flour
1 cup butter
2 tsp. ground cinnamon
½ cup sugar
3 eggs
1 tsp. salt
1 Tbs. grated orange rind
1 Tbs. grated lemon rind
½ cup coarsely chopped nuts
½ cup seedless raisins
2 Tbs. chopped glacé cherries
Confectioners' sugar and water frosting
Glacé cherries, angelica and toasted blanched almonds
½ square (½ oz.) semisweet chocolate, melted

Soften yeast in lukewarm water 5 minutes. Heat milk to boiling point and cool to lukewarm. Add to softened yeast along with 1 cup of the flour and beat well. Cover and let stand 30 minutes. Cream butter until soft and fluffy. Add cinnamon and sugar gradually. Beat in 3 eggs, one at a time. Add the yeast mixture and beat again. Stir in salt and remaining flour to make a soft, easily handled dough. Knead on a lightly floured board until smooth and elastic (at least 10 minutes) and place in a greased bowl. Turn once to coat with grease. Cover and let rise 1½ hours or until doubled in bulk. On a lightly floured board, knead in orange and lemon rinds, nuts, raisins and cherries. Divide the dough in half and form each half into a long, narrow roll. Join the ends of each roll to form a circle and place on a greased baking sheet. Cover and let rise until doubled in bulk. Then, with a very sharp knife, make tiny slashes in the top of the crown, about 2 inches apart. Bake in preheated hot oven (400°F.) about 20 minutes. Cool. Frost with confectioners' sugar and water frosting. Garnish with glacé cherries, angelica and whole almonds dipped in melted chocolate.

Confectioners' sugar and water frosting: Stir about 4 teaspoons water into 1 cup sifted confectioners' sugar.

Makes 2 coffee rings, 12 to 13 inches in diameter.

Pan de Lucía
Lucía's Easter Egg Bread
Another traditional favorite and an unusual and delicious treat for friends.

4 envelopes active dry yeast	1 Tbs. coarsely ground black pepper
4 cups warm water (110° to 115°F.)	¼ lb. finely diced salt pork (fat back)
¼ cup sugar	12 raw whole eggs
2 Tbs. salt	
12 to 13 cups flour	

Soften yeast in 2 cups of the warm water (not hot); add sugar and salt and remaining warm water. Stir in 8 to 9 cups of the flour. Work in remaining flour with the hands. Knead dough at least 10 minutes, or until smooth and satiny. Place in an ungreased bowl. Cover with a clean towel. Let rise in a warm place (80° to 85°F.) until double in bulk. Punch down dough. Sprinkle with black pepper and finely diced pork. Work it into the dough until thoroughly blended. Save a piece of dough, about ¼ of the batch, for later use. Shape remaining dough into 2 large rings on a greased and lightly floured baking sheet. Make 6 holes in the top of each ring, spaced equal distances apart. Insert a whole uncooked egg (do not break eggs) into each hole. Roll reserved dough into rectangle ¼ inch thick. Cut into 24 strips ½ inch wide. Place 2 strips in crisscross fashion over each egg. Cover and let dough rise until double in bulk, about 1 hour. Bake in a preheated hot oven (about 425°F.) 10 minutes. Reduce heat to moderate (350°F.) and bake 30 minutes or until done. To serve, cut bread and serve each person one egg.

Makes 12 servings.

Acapulco Fruit Compote

¾ cup water	2 qts. mixed cut-up fresh fruits such as cantaloupe, strawberries, watermelon, bananas, orange sections, peaches
⅓ cup sugar	
Peelings (yellow portion only) from 1 lemon	
3½ Tbs. lemon juice	
2 Tbs. pure vanilla extract	Vanilla ice cream or whipped cream
2 Tbs. orange liqueur (optional)	

In a small saucepan combine water, sugar and lemon peelings. Bring to boiling point; reduce heat and simmer for 2 minutes; cool. Strain. Add lemon juice, vanilla extract and orange liqueur. In a large serving bowl place fruits (in layers if desired). Pour syrup over fruit. Cover and refrigerate for 1 hour or until chilled. Serve as fruit cup or over ice cream or topped with vanilla whipped cream.

Makes 2 quarts fruit compote.

Pudín de Naranja
Orange Pudding
Where it's easy to get oranges we can expect some imaginative recipes. Here is one of them.

1½ cups cubed day-old bread	2 egg yolks
1 cup diced orange sections	1½ cups milk
⅔ cup sugar	2 Tbs. butter
1 Tbs. cornstarch	1 tsp. grated orange rind
¼ tsp. salt	1 tsp. pure vanilla extract
½ tsp. ground nutmeg	Meringue (see below)

Place bread cubes and orange segments in a 1-quart casserole and set aside. Combine sugar, cornstarch, salt and nutmeg in a saucepan. Blend in egg yolks and ¼ cup of the milk. Mix in remaining milk. Stir and cook over very low heat until custard coats a metal spoon and thickens slightly, about 10 minutes. Add butter, orange rind and vanilla extract to custard. Pour into the casserole, over bread cubes and orange sections. Place in a pan of hot water. Bake in preheated slow oven (325°F.) 1½ hours or until pudding is firm in center. Cover with meringue. Bake pudding 20 minutes longer in slow oven (300°F.) until meringue is brown. Serve warm.

Meringue: Add ⅛ teaspoon salt to 2 egg whites at room temperature. Beat until soft peaks form when the beater is lifted. Beat in 4 tablespoons sugar, 1 at a time. Continue beating until stiff peaks form when beater is lifted. Beat in ¼ teaspoon pure vanilla extract.

Makes 6 servings.

Acapulco Fruit Compote.

Flan Sabroso
Spicy Pumpkin Custard

You'll forget all about calories when you enjoy this super dessert.

¾ cup brown sugar, firmly packed	⅓ cup water
½ tsp. salt	1½ tsp. pure vanilla extract
1 tsp. ground cinnamon	Caramel (see below)
1 cup mashed cooked pumpkin	½ cup heavy cream, whipped
5 eggs, lightly beaten	1 Tbs. sugar
1½ cups undiluted evaporated milk	¼ tsp. ground ginger

Combine brown sugar, salt and cinnamon. Add pumpkin and beaten eggs and mix well. Stir in evaporated milk, water and vanilla extract, blending thoroughly. Make caramel coating for 8×8×2-inch pan as directed below. Pour pumpkin custard into caramel coated pan and set in larger pan of hot water. Bake in preheated moderate oven (350°F.) 1 hour 20 minutes or until a knife inserted in the center comes out clean. Remove from oven. Cool and chill. To serve, run a spatula around the sides of the pan and turn out on serving plate. Cut into 9 squares. Top with whipped cream sweetened with 1 tablesoon sugar and ¼ teaspoon ground ginger.

Caramel: Melt ½ cup sugar over medium low heat until it forms a golden syrup, stirring constantly to prevent burning. Pour immediately into baking pan, turning and tilting the pan from side to side to coat with caramel. Set aside to use later.

Makes 9 servings.

Plátanos en Salsa
Bananas in Rum Sauce

6 large ripe bananas	½ tsp. pure vanilla extract
¼ cup melted butter	
3 Tbs. rum	2 Tbs. confectioners' sugar

Peel bananas and cut each into 2 lengthwise slices. Sauté in hot butter. Drain on paper towels. Cool. Place bananas in a serving dish. Blend vanilla with rum and pour over bananas. Sprinkle with confectioners' sugar. Serve cold as a dessert. If desired, top with vanilla ice cream.

Makes 6 servings.

Sounds good

Plátanos Sabrosos
Spiced Baked Bananas

Still another way of serving up that favorite fruit—the banana.

3 large, firm bananas	¼ tsp. ground nutmeg
1½ Tbs. lime or lemon juice	Dash of ground cloves
3 Tbs. sugar	½ tsp. grated orange rind
¼ tsp. ground cinnamon	¼ cup orange juice
	1 Tbs. butter

Peel bananas, cut in half, crosswise, and then into lengthwise halves. Dip in lime juice and place in a 10×6×2-inch glass baking dish. Pour all remaining juice over bananas. Combine sugar with spices, grated orange rind and juice. Pour over bananas. Dot with butter. Bake in a preheated moderate oven (350°F.) 20 minutes. Serve as dessert or accompaniment to meat or poultry dishes.

Makes 6 servings.

Dulce de Jicama y Piña
Pineapple and Sweet Potato Pudding

The sweet potato again! Another good team, this time with crushed pineapple.

4 cooked medium-sized potatoes (1 lb.)	1 cup sugar
2 cups canned crushed pineapple, undrained	Cinnamon

Cook, peel and put sweet potatoes through coarse sieve (or blender) to make 2 cups puree. Combine with crushed pineapple with its liquid and sugar. Cook mixture over low heat, stirring, until the liquid has evaporated. Pour the pudding into a dish and serve sprinkled with cinnamon.

Makes 6 to 8 servings.

Spiced Baked Bananas.

Arroz con Leche
Tropical Rice with Milk

Mention "rice with milk" to most people and they are apt to think of a schoolroom menu. This recipe is far from it.

1 cup shredded coconut	2 sticks cinnamon
1½ cups milk	½ cup sugar
⅔ cup long-grained raw rice	¼ tsp. salt
1 cup boiling water	2 eggs, lightly beaten
	Raisins (optional)

Mix coconut with milk and heat 1 minute or until warm. Cook rice in boiling water along with cinnamon until all the liquid has been absorbed. Add coconut milk, sugar and salt. Continue cooking over low heat until rice is tender. Add a little of the hot mixture to the beaten egg. Then gradually add to remaining rice. Cook only until hot, 2 to 3 minutes. Serve hot, sprinkled with raisins, if desired.

Makes 4 to 6 servings.

The ingredients for Arroz con Leche *and the end result.*

Flan
Caramel Custard

This is a popular dessert in Mexico as well as Spain and all over South America. It's so good, in fact, that it has become almost an international favorite. In France you will find it listed as *Crème Caramel* and it has even found its way into the menus of India, Nepal and Sri Lanka.

Caramel

2 Tbs. water	½ cup sugar

Place 6 custard cups (or a 6-cup mold) in hot water to preheat. Place sugar and water in a small, 2-cup saucepan. Stir constantly over moderate heat until sugar has melted and mixture turns a golden brown. Quickly dry custard cups or mold and pour in caramel mixture, gently turning dishes until the inside is coated.

Custard

4 cups milk	⅛ tsp. salt
8 eggs, lightly beaten	¾ cup sugar
	1 tsp. vanilla

Preheat oven to 350°F. (moderate). Scald milk in 2-quart saucepan. Beat eggs with a rotary beater. Continue to beat while adding sugar gradually. If you add it too quickly, it won't dissolve. Add hot milk to egg mixture slowly, beating constantly. Beat in vanilla and salt. Strain mixture through cheesecloth and divide into caramelized cups or pour into mold. Place in pan of hot water so that water level reaches half the depth of the cups or mold.

Bake in preheated oven for 30 minutes (1 hour if using 6-cup mold) and cook until the blade of a knife inserted in the center comes out clean. Let cool at room temperature and then chill in refrigerator several hours or overnight. To unmold, run a knife or spatula around the edges. Place a serving dish on top and invert to remove the flan.

Makes 6 servings.

Tip: Always add hot milk *slowly* to beaten eggs. Pouring too hastily may result in a nice dish of scrambled eggs. Some cooks feel they

The most typically Mexican of all desserts, flan.

can help avoid this catastrophe by adding a teaspoon of cornstarch to eggs before adding a hot liquid. For variation, instead of vanilla, try adding 2 tablespoons sweetened cocoa mix or ½ teaspoon powdered cinnamon.

Sounds good!

Parfait de Chocolate
Chocolate Parfait

Chocolate is a favorite flavor in almost every place, especially in Mexico.

1 square (1 oz.) unsweetened chocolate	3 egg whites, beaten
½ tsp. ground cinnamon	1½ tsp. pure vanilla extract
⅔ cup sugar	2 cups heavy cream, whipped
¾ cup water	

Grate chocolate and blend with cinnamon and set aside. Bring sugar and water to boiling point and cook without stirring for 5 minutes. Gradually beat syrup into beaten egg whites and continue beating until mixture cools. Fold in grated chocolate and cinnamon mixture, vanilla extract and whipped cream. Turn into 2 ice-cube trays and freeze until firm and ready to serve.

Makes 8 servings.

Buñuelos

No matter whether you call them by their Spanish name or just plain fritters, they are equally good.

⅔ cup flour	1 egg, slightly beaten
1 tsp. sugar	Fat for frying
¼ tsp. salt	

Mix flour, sugar and salt. Add beaten egg and mix to very stiff dough. Knead for a minute, adding more flour if needed to keep dough from sticking. Cut bits of dough the size of walnuts and roll paper thin on floured board. Heat fat for frying (should be at least an inch deep in pan) to about 390°F. or hot enough for a 1-inch cube of bread to brown in 20 seconds. Fry *buñuelos* one at a time, dunking each under hot fat as soon as it is put in kettle. If fat is the right temperature, the dough will blister

and puff up like a big potato chip. Fry until golden brown. Drain on paper towels and dust liberally with cinnamon and confectioners' sugar. Or serve as a dessert with honey, jam or ice cream.

Makes 6 to 8.

Churros
Mexican Crullers

Churros to the Mexicans are what doughnuts are to us. Sometimes a dessert and very often a *merienda,* or snack, they are often served with a cup of hot chocolate but taste just as delicious with coffee.

Lard or oil for frying	1½ cups boiling water
1 slice stale white bread	1 large egg, unbeaten
½ lemon	Powdered sugar
1½ cups flour	
1 tsp. salt	

Before preparing batter, heat lard or oil in a large pan. Add bread and lemon to hot fat and remove when bread is a very dark brown. This adds a distinctive flavor to the fat. In a mixing bowl blend flour and salt; make a well in the center, add boiling water and mix well. When dough is light and smooth, add egg and continue to beat until mixture is shiny. (Unless your right arm is extrastrong, we suggest you use an electric mixer.) Reheat the fat to 375°F. Pour batter a small amount at a time into a pastry bag with a plain tube. For each cruller squeeze about 2 tablespoons of the batter into the hot fat. Remove when golden brown all over and drain on paper towels. Repeat until all batter is used. While still hot, roll in powdered sugar and serve hot.

Makes approximately 6 to 8 servings.

Pasteles de Canela
Cinnamon Cookies

This is a favorite recipe, since both cinnamon and cookies are very popular.

2 cups flour	½ cup finely chopped walnuts
1½ cups sifted confectioners' sugar, divided	1 tsp. pure vanilla extract
3 tsp. ground cinnamon, divided	1 cup softened butter

In a mixing bowl blend flour, ½ cup confectioners' sugar and 2 teaspoons of the cinnamon. Add walnuts and stir in vanilla. Work in butter with fork or pastry blender until mixture resembles coarse cornmeal; press together to form a ball. Shape dough with hands into ½-inch balls; flatten slightly. Place 1 inch apart on ungreased cookie sheet. Bake in a preheated moderate oven (350°F.) 30 minutes or until lightly browned. In a small bowl combine remaining 1 cup confectioners' sugar with the remaining 1 teaspoon cinnamon. Dredge cookies while still warm with cinnamon-sugar mixture. Cool and dredge again.

Makes 4 dozen.

Cáscara de Fruta
Candied Fruit Peel

Not strictly a dessert, but a wonderful nibble.

Peel of 4 large oranges, 2 grapefruits or 6 limes	1 Tbs. salt 2 cups sugar

Peel citrus carefully, discarding white membrane, which is inclined to be bitter. Cut in ¼-inch strips and soak overnight in water to cover and salt. Next day drain thoroughly and wash peel in fresh water. Cover peel with cold water and bring slowly to boiling. Drain. Repeat boiling 3 times, using fresh cold water each time. Drain thoroughly. Add sugar to peel. Add a little water and stir to dissolve sugar. Cook slowly until peel is translucent. Drain if necessary. Turn in granulated sugar. Dry on wire rack and store in airtight container.

Leche Quemada sin Trabajo
Burned Milk without Work

The literal translation of the name of this candy does not sound too appetizing, but it is actually a delicious and easy-to-make dish. All you need is time and patience.

1 can (14 oz.) sweetened condensed milk

Place unopened can of milk in deep saucepan. Cover can with hot water, bring to a boil and then reduce heat to simmer. Continue to simmer for 2½ to 3 hours, while adding boiling water to keep the can covered. Remove can from water and cool. Remove contents onto a serving dish and chill in refrigerator.

Makes 6 servings.

A steaming cup of hot chocolate, with the main ingredient in two forms.

12
Beverages

Mexican Hot Chocolate

Especially good in cool weather, cocoa and cinnamon make a delightful twosome.

¼ cup sugar
¼ cup unsweetened cocoa
½ tsp. ground cinnamon
Dash of ground nutmeg

½ cup water
1 quart milk
1 egg white, unbeaten

Mix sugar, cocoa, cinnamon and nutmeg. Blend in water. Boil 1 minute. Beat milk and egg white together only until blended; stir into the chocolate syrup. Cook until hot (do not boil), beating constantly with a rotary beater. Serve hot.
Makes 6 servings.

Garapiña

This is a very good and refreshing beverage. The amount of hot water depends on the size of the bowl and the amount of pineapple peelings.

Pineapple peelings from 1 medium-
  sized fresh pineapple
Hot water to cover, about 4 cups

½ cup sugar
½ cup fresh lemon juice

Wash pineapple peelings well in warm water. Place in a bowl. Add hot water to cover, the amount depending upon the size and shape of the bowl. Cover and let stand 24 hours. Strain. Add sugar and lemon juice. Chill and serve.
Makes 1 quart.

Vanilla Coffee Liqueur

Delicious as a liqueur or in cold milk or as a sauce for ice cream, puddings or over sliced ripe bananas.

1½ cups brown sugar, firmly packed
  1 cup granulated sugar

2 cups water
½ cup instant coffee powder

Sangría *in a pitcher.*

3 cups vodka   ½ vanilla bean, split, *or* 2 Tbs. pure vanilla extract

Combine sugars with water. Bring to boil and boil for 5 minutes. Gradually stir in coffee, using a wire whisk. Cool. Pour into a jar or jug. Add vodka and vanilla. Mix thoroughly. Cover and let stand at least 2 weeks. Remove bean. If extract is used, liqueur may be used immediately.

Makes about 5 cups.

Sangría

Sangría is a cooling drink that originated in Spain but is now popular in Mexico and South America. It can be as alcoholic or as temperate as you wish, and since most Latinos are very temperate, you might wish to add extra Cointreau or some Spanish brandy. A standard version of *sangría* consists of a bottle of red wine (1 pint 7 oz. size) mixed with 2 tablespoons sugar, a sliced lemon and ½ orange, sliced. When the sugar has dissolved, add 2 ounces orange juice (or Cointreau) and 12 ounces club soda. Chill well or serve in a large pitcher with ice cubes. *Or* combine a quart of dry red wine with 2 cans (6 oz.) frozen limeade that have been reconstituted and a 28-ounce bottle of club soda. Pour over ice cubes in a large pitcher and garnish with orange slices.

Makes a refreshing drink for 4.

Margarita

The *margarita* is a popular way of serving tequila—as an alternative to drinking it "as is," with salt to taste, poured on the hand. The inside rim of a cocktail glass is rubbed with a slice of lime and then dipped in salt, which adheres to the seasoned glass. Combine 5 jiggers tequila with ½ jigger of Triple Sec, 2½ jiggers lime juice and 3 or 4 ice cubes. Shake well in a large pitcher and then strain into each prepared cocktail glass.

Makes 4 servings.

A glass prepared with a salted edge for a margarita.

Sources of Supply

Gebhardt's Mexican Foods
P.O. Box 7130
Station "A"
San Antonio, Texas 78285

Old El Paso
Mountain Pass Canning Co.
Anthony, Texas 88021

V. F. Garza & Sons, Inc.
910 East Chicago Avenue
East Chicago, Indiana 46312

Casa Moneo
210 West 14th Street
New York, New York 10011

Index

Almond Sauce, 74
    Fish in, 47
    Meatballs in, 59
Appetizers, 21, 25
Avocado, 12
    Salad, Stuffed, 76
    Soup, 28
    Stuffed, 77, 78

Bananas
    Rum Sauce over, 82
    Spiced Baked, 82
    Sweet Potatoes and, 72
Batter, 68
Bean
    Enchiladas, 37
    Salad, Green, 76
    Soup, Lima, 28
Beans, 10
    with Cheese, Kidney, 66
    Refried, 10, 65
    Sausage and, 58
    Tostados and Chorizo with, 41
Beef
    Chili con Carne and, 63
    Tacos, 38, 39
Beverages, 16
Bread
    Lucía's Easter Egg, 80
    Onion Corn, 45
Buñuelos, 15, 86

Cake, Three Kings Coffee, 79
Caramel, 84
Carrots with Cumin, Diced, 66
Casserole
    Meat, 57
    Spiced Pumpkin, 70
    Tamale, 44
Cheese, 12
    Chili with, 64
    Kidney Beans and, 66
    Soup, 29
Chick Peas, 11
    Salad, 78
    Soup, 28

Chicken
    Broth, 27
    with Chili, 64
    Corn Salad and, 55
    Enchiladas, 36
    Fricassee with Almonds, 54
    Fricassee with Sesame Seeds, 53
    Mexican Style, 54
    Rice and, 52
    Stew, María's, 53
Chili, 8, 9, 10
    Barry Goldwater's, 62
    con Carne, 61
    con Carne with Beef and Ham, 63
    con Carne, Eisenhower, 62
    con Carne, Havasu, 63
    with Cheese, 64
    Cheese-stuffed Potatoes and, 70
    with Chicken, 64
    Nixon, 62
    Pedernales River, 62
    Pork Stew from Puebla, 57
    Powder, 61
    Quiche, 34
    Sauce and Shrimp Fritters, 48
    Sauce, Red, 75
    Tacos, 38
    Texas Jailhouse, 61
Chocolate, 13
    Mexican Hot, 89
    Parfait, 86
Chorizo with Tostados and Refried Beans, 41
Compote, Acapulco Fruit, 80
Condiments, 28
Cookies, Cinnamon, 86
Corn, 7, 35
    Bread, Onion, 45
    Flour, 8
    Salad and Chicken, 55
    Sauté, Mexican, 67
    Soup, 27
    Zucchini and, Mexican, 67
Crullers, Mexican, 86
Custard
    Caramel, 84
    Spicy Pumpkin, 82

Desserts, 79
Dough
    Basic Tamale, 42
    Quesadilla, 41

Eggs, 32
    Chapultepec, 33
    Country Style, 32
    Malaga Style, 33
    San Luis Potosi Style, 34
    Scrambled, 32
    Shrimp and, 33
Enchiladas, 15
    Bean, 37
    Chicken, 36
    Swiss, 37
    Tampico Style, 36
Equipment, Kitchen, 6

Festival Foods, 16
Filling
    Quesadilla, 41
    Tacos, 38
    Tamale, 43
    Tostados, 40
Fish, 13, 46
    Sauces for, 46, 47
Fritters
    Buñuelos, 86
    Onion, 68
    Shrimp, with Savory Sauce, 47
Fruit
    Compote, Acapulco, 80
    Peel, Candied, 87

Garapiña, 89
Green Bean Salad, 76
Guacamole, 21

Ham with Chili con Carne, 63
Herbs, 14

Kidney Beans with Cheese, 66

Lent, Tostados for, 41
Lima Bean Soup, 28
Liqueur, Vanilla Coffee, 89
Little Meats, 24

Margarita, 91
Meat, 13, 56
    Casserole, 57
    Loaf, Mexican, 59
    Meatball Soup, 29
    Meatballs in Almond Sauce, 59
    Stuffing, 68

Meats, Little, 24
Milk
    Burned, without Work, 87
    Tropical Rice and, 84
Mole Sauces, 15, 50, 51
Mushrooms with Tacos, 25

Nuts, 12

Onion
    Corn Bread, 45
    Fritters, 68
Orange
    Pudding, 80
    Sauce with Fish, 46

Parfait, Chocolate, 86
Pastry, Turnover, 24
Peppers, 9
    Stuffed, 68
Picadillo, Party, 58
Pie, Tamale, 44
Pineapple and Sweet Potato Pudding, 82
Plantains, 12
    Stuffed, 68
Pork
    Durango, 56
    Stew from Puebla, Chili, 57
Potatoes, Chili Cheese-stuffed, 70
Poultry, 50
Pudding
    Orange, 80
    Sweet Potato, 82
Pumpkin Casserole, Spiced, 70

Quesadillas, 15, 41
Quiche, Chili, 34

Rice, 11
    Chicken and, 52
    Drunken Turkey and, 52
    Mexican Style, 30
    Tropical, with Milk, 84
Rolls, Miniature Stuffed, 25
Rosca de Reyes, 17. *See also* Cake
Rum Sauce, Bananas in, 82

Salad, 73
    Avocado, Stuffed, 76
    Caesar, 75
    Chick Pea, 78
    Corn, and Chicken, 55
    Green Bean, 76
    Mexican, 48
    Shrimp, 48

Sandwiches, Mexican, 26
Sangría, 16, 91
Sauce, 73
  Almond, 74
  Almond, with Fish, 47
  Almond, with Meatballs, 59
  Chili, for Shrimp Fritters, 48
  Country Style, 74
  Fish and, 47
  Green, 74
  Mexican, for Shrimp, 48
  Mole, 15, 50, 51
  Red Chili, 75
  Rum, Bananas in, 82
  Tomato, 39, 73
  Tomato, Uncooked, 74
Sausage
  Beans and, 58
  Spanish, 30
Seasoning, 6
Sesame Seeds with Chicken Fricassee, 53
Shrimp
  Eggs and, 33
  Fritters with Savory Sauce, 47
  Mexican Sauce on, 48
  Salad, 48
Soup, 11, 27, 30
  Avocado, 28
  Cheese, 29
  Chick Pea, 28
  Corn, 27
  Lima Bean, 28
  Meatball, 29
  Squash, Mexican Style, 31
  Tortilla, 31
  with Vermicelli and Spanish Sausage, 30
Spanish Sausage, 30
Spices, 14
Spinach, Savory, 70
Squash
  Soup, Mexican Style, 31
  Stuffed Small, 72
Stew
  Chili Pork from Puebla, 57
  María's Chicken
Stuffing, Meat, 68
Sweet Potato
  Bananas and, 72
  Pudding, and Pineapple, 82
  Rumba, 71

Tacos, 14, 37
  Beef, 38, 39
  Chili, 38
  Filling, 38
  Green, Red, and White, 39
  Mushrooms and, 25
Tamales, 15, 42, 43
  Casserole, 44
  Dough, Basic, 42
  Filling for, 43
  Pie, 44
  Sweet, 44
Tomato Sauce, 39, 73, 74
Tortilla, 7, 14, 35
  Dry Soup, 31
  North Americans', 35
Tostados, 40
  Fillings for, 40
  Lenten, 41
  Refried Beans, Chorizos, and, 41
  Pastry, 24
Turkey
  in Mole Sauce, 50
  Rice and, 52
Turnover. *See also* Quesadillas

Vanilla, 14
Vegetables, 65
Vermicelli, 30

Zucchini
  Mexican Corn and, 67
  Mexican Style, 72

Chicken anchile p. 36